LAURA CERETA
QUATTROCENTO
HUMANIST

medieval & renaissance texts & studies

1. Frank Livingstone Huntley, *Bishop Joseph Hall and Protestant Meditation in Seventeenth-Century England: A Study, With the Texts of The Art of Divine Meditation (1606) and Occasional Meditations (1633).*

2. *Johannes de Alta Silva, Dolopathos: or The King and the Seven Wise Men.* Translated by Brady B. Gilleland.

3. Albert Rabil, Jr., *Laura Cereta: Quattrocento Humanist.*

Laura Cereta
Quattrocento Humanist

BY

Albert Rabil Jr.

medieval & renaissance texts & studies
Center for Medieval & Early Renaissance Studies
Binghamton, New York
1981

Publication of this book was generously aided by State University of New York at Old Westbury.

This book is published in both clothbound and paperbound editions.

ISBN 0-86698-002-4 *(cloth)*
ISBN 0-86698-007-5 *(paper)*

Center for Medieval and Early Renaissance Studies
State University of New York at Binghamton

this book is dedicated to my parents

Sophie Mae Rabil

Albert Rabil, Sr.

with gratitude and love

Preface

What follows is a critical study of the life and work of Laura Cereta (the first ever attempted), a calendar and summary of her entire corpus, and critical texts of the twelve items in that corpus never before published. Taken together, these three parts of the study are intended to contribute to the analysis of the role of women in Renaissance Humanism and to provide critical tools for the examination of Cereta's work and its place in Italian Humanism.

The study was begun during a sabbatical leave, 1977–78. I am grateful for the leave and for the opportunity to spend the year in Italy, especially Florence. Librarians in a number of cities were most cooperative in helping me track down materials and in making their facilities available. I would particularly like to thank those who assisted me at the Queriniana in Brescia, the Riccardiana in Florence, the Marciana in Venice, and the Vatican in Rome.

The study completed in Italy is Part One of this book. During the research and writing of that part, I was constantly helped by the advice of Professors Margaret King of Brooklyn College and Paul Kristeller of Columbia University. Professor Kristeller later suggested that a critical text of the unpublished materials in the Cereta corpus should be prepared. These now comprise Part Three, and I am deeply indebted to Professor Kristeller for help rendered on many difficult problems related to those texts and for checking my transcription of the manuscript. I am also indebted to Professor Warren S. Smith Jr., Department of Classics, University of New Mexico, for many helpful suggestions related to Part Three, as well as for the analysis of the Latin style and vocabulary of Brother Thomas and Laura. Needless to say, I assume full responsibility for whatever errors remain in the text.

A question was raised as to whether to publish all the Cereta materials, including those published by Tomasini in 1640. Since these materials are available to those who might need them, and since that would have added considerably to the bulk of this volume, it was decided not to publish them again. However, in Part Two a complete analysis of Cereta's corpus includes a calendar as well as a summary of all extant materials, so that both the layman and the scholar may gain some idea of the scope and content of her work and possess a guide to its critical interpretation.

Throughout this study Laura Cereta is referred to as Cereta, in keeping with the common practice of referring to humanists by their last names. The only exception to this rule is that when her name appears in sentences in which the first names of others have been used, she is referred to as Laura. In order to facilitate comprehension of my interpretation and an understanding of the relation of various letters to one another, items are cross-referenced, usually to the chronological numbering followed in the summary of the works of Cereta in Part Two. Sometimes, however, when specific passages are referred to, the appropriate citation in the Tomasini edition or in Part Three of this volume is also noted.

I cannot close without a special word of thanks to my parents, to whom this book is dedicated, for their support and encouragement through this, as all, years, and to my wife and children who listened to Cereta's story until she became part of our family in Italy.

ALBERT RABIL, JR.

Westbury, New York
September, 1980

Contents

PART ONE

An Interpretation of the Life and Work of Laura Cereta

Introduction

Laura Cereta (1469–99), born into the Brescian nobility, learned Latin and Greek language and literature from her father.[1] Before her marriage to a local merchant at the age of fifteen, she was already composing Latin orations and letters in the manner of the humanists of her day. Left a widow and childless after just eighteen months of marriage, she threw herself with even greater vigor into her studies and exchanged letters with many learned persons, male and female, both within and beyond Brescia. According to a later tradition,[2] she presented philosophical theses publicly at the age of eighteen and from the age of twenty taught philosophy for seven consecutive years. In 1488 she edited her letters, dedicating them to Cardinal D. D. Ascanius Maria Sforza. Several manuscript copies were made, and some of the letters were finally published in 1640. We have nothing from her pen during the final eleven years of her life. She died suddenly of causes unknown in her thirtieth year and was buried in the cathedral amid great public acclamation and mourning, according to Brescia's first historian writing just five years after her death.[3]

During the first four centuries following her death a number of historians of Italian literature or biographers of Italian writers praised her, though only two of these analyzed her life and thought.[4] The remainder made passing references to her. For the most part they report that she wrote a volume of letters, and in some cases they offer one or another comment about her life or work, comments which quite often are not based on any primary source. Some of these conflict with others. Together they constitute a "secondary tradition" out of which the true and the false must be carefully sifted.[5] During the twentieth century there have been three articles devoted to her life and work, all by Brescian historians. Two of these are based on her published letters, while the third analyzes and publishes an unpublished manuscript letter.[6] She is also treated in the recent *Storia di Brescia.* What is said there is based on analyses written in the eighteenth century and the early part of this century, but its statements, even from these sources, are not always accurate.[7] Her life and thought, in short, have never been submitted to a systematic treatment based on all the extant sources. My intention in the following analysis is to fill this lacuna and to assess her place in Quattrocento humanism.

Early Childhood and Intellectual Formation

Cereta wrote three letters in which she discusses the details of her life: the prologue and epilogue to her collected letters addressed to Cardinal Ascanius Maria Sforza and an autobiographical letter written to, and at the request of a friend, Nazaria Olympia (84, 83, and 50 respectively). In addition, she makes passing comments in other letters that are valuable for a fuller interpretation of her early years.

Laura was the eldest of six children, born in late August or September 1469, to Silvester Cereta whose family came from a town by that name, and to Veronica di Leno of an old Brescian family. Her recollection is that she was cuddled and catered to by the entire household, a fact she attributes to her being the first-born child who, she says, is often the best loved (T pp. 146–47). It is significant that Cereta feels this way about herself at the age of seventeen (her age when she writes this letter to Nazaria Olympia). In a male-oriented culture she was not made to feel that she was of less value than her three brothers whose births followed hers. This explains in part her aggressiveness against those, male and female, who later attacked her.

The happiness of her very early years was marred only by frail health due to some long-lasting infection. She overcame this, however, by the age of seven when she was sent to a convent to live with nuns for two years. During her first year there she acquired the barest rudiments of reading and writing, and more importantly, she felt, the ability to discipline herself. For the rest, she describes sleepless nights spent embroidering, at which she became very adept (T pp. 148–49). During her second year she was instructed in religion and learned to be obedient, not only to the received doctrines of the faith, but to persons in authority over her.

After two years her father brought her back home, where she was welcomed with the same kind of love she had received before she left. Her father became her teacher, and the relationship between them remained close until his death. In her autobiographical letter she says that she was eleven when she began these more serious studies with her father (50; T p. 150). But in one letter written prior to this one, she says that she has devoted seven years to these studies, which would mean that she began when she was nine and one-half (33; T p. 74). And in a letter written subsequent to her autobiographical letter she asserts that envy had been kindled against her before she was ten years old (12; T p. 104).

She was drawn first to the study of mathematics (29, 2, and 50; T pp. 2, 20 and 150, respectively). Doubtless her great love for astrology and her desire to know the dimensions of the heavens comes from these years and helps to explain the prominence of this theme in a number of her early letters. Then she turned her attention to sacred literature. But philosophy became her surpassing passion. She expended herself on these studies, enchanted, she says, by the wonderful example of Petrarch (miro Petrarcae preconio cantatum, T p. 20). So great became her interest that she sacrificed her mathematical studies in order to pursue philosophy more avidly. In the same letter in which she says that she wishes to follow the example of Petrarch, she also expresses a desire to measure the distance of the earth from the stars Atlanta and Endymion (2; T p. 21). And in a letter written the following month, she asserts that she wants to obtain measurements from Helpericum and Albumasar in order to determine how far the planets are from one another and how far Saturn is from the stars (13; T p. 90). But ten months later she says that although Pythagoras wrote that the sun is eight times larger than the earth, and although other philosophers assert equally esoteric things, these are not questions for her to weigh (43; T pp. 80–81).

In her pursuit of humanist studies she developed a veritable passion to acquire immortality through her own literary efforts, a passion particularly pronounced in her earlier letters. Her earliest extant letter asserts that she expended herself on her studies in order to gain immortality (2; T p. 20). In a letter nearly contemporary with this one she says that the reward for knowledge is fame and that her only interest is in what will commend her name to eternity (4; II: 5–13). To a preacher, Brother Ludovico de la Turre, she asserts that she desires immortality through her letters just as he, because of his profession of religion, desires to see the face of God (12; T p. 105). In her autobiographical letter she says that prior to the crisis of her husband's death, she always sent forth her letters with a vigor that would exalt her throughout the land (50; T p. 146).

Cereta's training was primarily in Latin language and literature, and it was on this explicitly that her critics later sought to undermine her (7; T p. 122). But she also learned Greek; she uses Greek words in two of her letters (T 17 and 36) and refers to having received a letter which contained Greek as well as Latin from one of her correspondents (6; III: 3–6). Her Latin style is classical in form, certainly far from the relative simplicity of medieval Latin. In fact, her Latin is at times fairly complicated and overstylized, and although she is often clear enough, there are some passages where her meaning is difficult to grasp. The latter is true also because in some passages she seems to be speaking metaphorically or allusively about matters familiar to the correspondent but not to us. Moreover, although she adopts classical form in general, she does not hesitate to use words characteristic of medieval rather than of classical Latin and words that were unknown in classical Latin in the form in which she uses them. This is consistent with her view that the moderns know a great many things that were unknown to the ancients (T p. 222). She looks to the ancients for inspiration, but she remains self-consciously a modern in doing so. (For further analysis of her use of language, see Part Three, Introduction, below.)

Cereta's letters are full of classical allusions and citations from both Greek and Latin literature. Never, however, does she directly quote a classical writer. Her titled letters are especially full of these allusions and citations (see below, 21, 32, 47, 55, 56, 67, 77, and 82), though they appear everywhere. (See, e.g., 6, 14, 24, 35, 57, 60, 80, 81, and 83.) She is especially fond of drawing examples from history, and in doing so she mixes legendary figures (including gods and goddesses) with historical figures without distinction (see, e.g., 77). The letters reflect wide reading and memorizing of classical texts and examples.

Her classical learning is primarily literary, despite the fact that she calls it philosophy. What she perhaps intends is what the humanists meant by moral philosophy, for it is in the interest of an ethical rather than a systematically philosophical view of life that she draws on the literary tradition. She mentions the names of various philosophers from time to time, but the only philosopher whose views she actually discusses are those of Epicurus. About him she writes to her sister that he was a temperate and moderate man who did not think of pleasure as sheer enjoyment but rather as the freedom of a virtuous soul (76).

Although Cereta was trained in both sacred and secular literature, the classical citations far outweigh those from the religious tradition, reflecting the depth of the passion she developed for her classical studies. Her spiritual adviser, Brother Thomas, will accuse her, as we shall see, of being too classical and not Christian enough. For the most part, however, Cereta herself remained unconscious of any tension between these two. She was both a pious Christian and a humanist. Quite often in her letters references from both sacred and secular sources are placed side by side without any sense of misgiving. The most striking instance of this is in her letter to Bishop Paul Zane on the Eucharist (19; v: 13f). She cites, among others, the Romans who venerated the tablets of the law, the ark of the covenant, and the image of the Virgin; the pagans who, in their error, worshipped the relics of Danaus, as well as the mother of the gods, and the Sibylline books; the Roman Emperor Alexander who ordered the images of Virgil and Cicero to be kept on an altar; and Christians who honor wood from the cross and thorns of the Lord as household gods. There is one instance in which Cereta sets herself in relation to biblical rather than classical women (54), but by and large she reflects a naivete which is truly disarming. She does not ponder the relation between Christian and classical, for this did not present itself as a problem to her.

After Cereta had been pursuing her studies for only a year, she says in her autobiographical letter, she acquired virtually the complete management of domestic affairs so that, as she puts it, she grew old while she was still young (50; T p. 150). Her mother must therefore have been away, as she was when Cereta wrote to her on September 5, 1485 (14). At that time Cereta was already married, and she was in charge of a household which included her father's family as well as her husband (29; T p. 13). This situation is corroborated by the letter she wrote to John Olivieri on August 1, 1485, employing him to instruct her brothers Basil and Hippolytus (7). It is somewhat puzzling that Cereta rather than her father assumed this particular task. The situation did not persist, for two years later she wrote to a friend that she had been absent from her father for a long time (T p. 112). The details provided in the extant materials do not allow us to gain a clearer picture of her relationship to her family in this respect.

Be that as it may, Cereta did not allow her household duties to rob her of time necessary for studies. To make it up, she studied at night, reading and above all composing letters after everyone else had gone to bed. Sometimes she worked until nearly morning (29; T p. 13). However much others may surpass her in genius and learning, she writes, none surpasses her in diligence and in the fatigue brought on by study (64; T p. 102).

During these years of study, especially in its more advanced stages, Cereta was not isolated with her books and her father but participated in a wider society of learning. She refers several times in her letters to visits to Santa Clara (Chiara), a nearby monastery, for what appear to have been discussions of an intellectual nature. Some of the earliest criticisms of her work arose out of this circle (30 and 66; T pp. 40–42, and 81). Brescia during these years was beginning to enter fully into Renaissance culture. After the "German War" ended in 1487 the city knew twenty-five years of uninterrupted peace which modern historians of Brescia call "the golden age" of the Brescian Renaissance. A prominent school of art, printing presses (which produced many classical editions), schools, and learned groups began to flourish throughout the city.[8] Laura herself, together with her brother Daniel, participated in one such group, called the Mondella Academy after the name of the doctor in whose home the group met.[9] The many names of those who praised and criticized her, mentioned at various points in her letters, are a testimony to the wide diffusion of classical learning in the city.

Marriage and Its Impact on Her Life

Cereta was married at the age of fifteen, probably in December 1484 or January 1485. This, however, did not interrupt her studies. She gives every indication of having continued after that event, as before it, in pursuit of the Muses. Her husband, Peter Serina, though a merchant and inferior to her in education, was not without learning. Four letters to him are preserved, and they indicate that while away on business he wrote to her, perhaps also in Latin as she wrote to him. In her first letter to him she says that in her view he has a respected place in comparison with other men of learning, though she suggests at the same time that to his honor she could boast more about her own learning (3). She also mentions his learning in one of her many lamentations after his death saying that they were united together in a quiet zeal for letters and in an inviolable peace (51).

The relationship, however, to judge from the extant letters, was not always one of peace and concord. Peter was away during July, August, and September 1485 on a business trip to Venice. (Cereta began writing the letters she subsequently published in July 1485, probably as her husband was departing on this trip.) Letters written to him during these months suggest that they were having some difficulty relating to each other through correspondence. Either the silences were too long or what was said was not appropriate. Laura misses him a great deal (3 and 5; T pp. 23–25 and 26–27). He accused her of not loving him sufficiently, a charge which brought from her a letter expressing the hurt this caused her (11; IV). In her last letter, she is disturbed that his grief over his brother's death is so inconsolable (44; T pp. 21–22). The letters thus suggest that extended absence from one another was causing some strain in their relationship.

The last letter is poignant, referring as it does to the death of Peter's brother, Nicholas. For two weeks after she penned it, Peter himself died of a fever, perhaps while still at his paternal home mourning his brother. Cereta was sent for and arrived just in time to see her husband breathe his last. She mentions this moment twice (54 and 58; T pp. 66 and 61, respectively). In the first of these accounts she writes:

At last I came when my husband was feverish. Dying myself, I saw him half dead, I was pretty well deserted. I wept his death, I fell lifeless over his body, and the house which awaited me for marriage admitted me to mourning as a house of death. Thus one, and that an abominable year, saw me a girl, bride, widow, and deprived of all the goods of fortune.

(Veni tandem febriente marito: Hunc moribunda visi [sic] seminecem, solavi [sic] meliusculum, flevi defunctum, cecidi super cadaver exanimis, et quae me expectabat ad nuptias, ad planctum funesta domus admisit. Sic unus, infandusque annus me Puellam vidit, Sponsam, Viduam, atque omnibus Fortunae bonis orbatam, T p. 66).

Cereta, who by her own confession had hardly gotten to know her husband while he was alive (58: T p. 61), got to know herself much more deeply through his death. She describes the progression of her life after her husband's death in one of the last letters she wrote. First she wept miserably and was inconsolable. Then she took refuge in religion. Finally, she turned to literature (79). This progression is detailed in various letters written during each of these periods or emotional states. For about a month she expressed a longing for death (46, 47, and 48; T pp. 58, 55–56, and 57, respectively), but then she took her own advice to her husband and pulled herself together. First, as she says, she did this through religion. Her raging grief was mitigated by the more certain hope that in the resurrected life she would meet her husband once again just as he was (67; T p. 141). She was also doubtless instructing herself when she wrote to a friend, consoling him on the death of his infant daughter, that if he would bear in mind that her death was part of a divine plan he would be able to restrain his weeping (52; T pp. 93–94). Thus she decided that her own longing would not be for death, but for God (49; T p. 115).

Her grief and her consolation in the face of it explain the change in her attitude toward astrology and fate. In the happier period preceding her husband's death, she penned a number of precise and elaborate descriptions of the positions of the heavens at particular times, because she believed that these positions were a portent of the present or future which could be known with greater certainty by these means. Thus in her letter to John Olivieri, the heavens at that moment (when Basil and Daniel, her brothers, were going to him for instruction) were favorable for learning arts and letters thoroughly

(39; T pp. 11–12). In two other letters she asserts that the positions of the heavens at one's birth are particularly important for understanding one's life, and she ventures a number of conclusions to be drawn from certain arrangements of the heavens (24 and 32; T pp. 127–29; and see also Part Two, Table of Extant Materials, with a note which adds a passage missing in T 64). In still another letter she suggests that through a knowledge of the heavens one gains a clearer understanding of the nature of God (38; T p. 29). In this connection, there is a remarkable letter to Brother Thomas of Florence, whom she had heard proclaim in a sermon that the order of nature is beyond our comprehension. Without denying his viewpoint, she nonetheless suggests to him that this is in profound contradiction to her own efforts to measure the heavens (13; T pp. 90–91).

All this changes after her husband's death. In her autobiographical letter she asserts that once delighted by these studies of the heavens, she now has lost interest in depicting secondary causes. One and the same eternal God, she says, is omnipotent. For this reason, the examination of the future is more characteristic of a rash curiosity than it is of a faithful mind (50; T pp. 152–53).

Her turn toward religion also altered, at least temporarily, her passion for attaining immortality through her pen. Writing two months after her husband's death she says that since this mortal life will be conquered by death, she has renounced the brief and fallen glory of the earth which separates us from true religion and causes us to yearn more for earthly fame than for eternal life (49; T pp. 115–16).

But after a relatively brief period of time, her preoccupation with religion gave way to a renewed dedication to and enthusiasm for studies. (There is a recapitulation here, however unconscious, of her early intellectual development, which began with sacred studies before she proceeded to classical studies.) Writing only three months after she had expressed a longing for death, she says that now only love of letters rages in her heart (51; T p. 157). She no longer believes the Muses are with her, and she regards her style as having degenerated from its former purity (50; T p. 146). Still she struggles and, according to her own words, it was not by crying but by reason that she finally rose above her anguish (57; T p. 60). The wound remained and would, she believed, always remain (50; T p. 151), but through study and correspondence she was prevailing.

With this renewed dedication to letters her earlier self-confidence and passion for immortality reasserted themselves, though in tones reflecting the tribulations through which she had passed. This is evident particularly in the epilogue and prologue to her epistles, the latest extant letters we have from her pen, both addressed to Cardinal Ascanius Maria Sforza. She admits that there are shortcomings in her work and that she is dedicating her letters to him because his authority will silence her critics. But she also believes that these letters will bring honor to his name in future generations. This was an attitude which places Cereta in the mainstream of humanism in Quattrocento Italy.

Cereta's identity as a humanist intellectual prevailed over her internal vicissitudes and, as we shall now see, over those created by the envy of her peers as well.

Controversies

In the prologue to her letters Cereta says that "it is rare to come upon a girl in any age who has written books with a refined elegance" ("quum rara inveniatur omni aevo puella quae libros accurata nitoris elegantia condiderit," T p. 6). It must have been so, for some of Cereta's most outstanding male correspondents raised questions about it, reflected in her earliest letters. Michael Baetus, a philosopher, questioned whether her descriptions of the heavens were not borrowed from some book (VIII: 1–3). Cereta concedes to him that she has learned much from the ancients, but argues that what she says is not borrowed from anyone, for she herself is an astrologer. She challenges him to find the book from which she has copied. To prove her point she appends to this letter, dated July 6, a description of the first four days of July (VIII: 17–39). John Olivieri, to whom she had written one of these descriptions (39) and at least one other letter as well (7), began to believe her critics, for apparently he sent his wife to visit Cereta and to obtain from her on the spot a Latin letter. Cereta, in obliging, says she did not expect this request but that she is happy to fulfill it. She adds, however, that she suspects a spy has been sent to determine the extent of her education. Do not, she exhorts, believe false disciples. Every person should be judged by the products of her intellect and not by the assaults of jealous critics.

And what was the assault? That Cereta's letters had been written, not by her, but by her father (70; T p. 84). The rumor must have been pursued by her enemies, for in three letters preceding her "performance" for Olivieri's wife, she mentions some of her critics by name. The first letter to mention the charge is addressed to Frontonus Carito on July 1, 1487, and begins with the statement: "You write that Eusebius read my letters and judged them to be not really mine but my father's" ("Quod scribis Eusebium legisse litteras meas, quas Patris judicavit esse, non proprias," T pp. 111–12). She also mentions Orosius as sharing Eusebius' view. On August 22, 1487 she mentions other critics: "Gismunda [Cassandra] abuses me because she believes that what I wrote came not from me but from the father who taught me" ("Dat igitur probro Gismunda [Cassandra, Vt] quod non mea, sed ejus, qui me instituit, patris credit esse quae scripsi," T p. 119). In this same letter Orosius, Orestes, and Phronicus are mentioned as part of this common crowd.

Evidently this was the culmination of rumors that had been circulating for some time. For Cereta says in her prologue that for a good while she withstood the taunts and did not respond (it was actually about six months), but that at last she could hold back no longer (84; T p. 4). When she finally did speak, it was with an unrestrained rage. On July 1, 1487, she penned her invective against Orestes and Phronicus in which she easily returned in kind what had been said about her. What have I done, she asks, that you should "vomit forth muddy opinions from the bilgewater of envy? Would that even once you had listened to Cicero speaking or Livy reciting or Plato treating of immortality" ("coenosas evomueris de sentina invidentiae sentenias: utinam saltem vel semel orantem Tullium, aut legentem Livium, vel disserentem audivisses de immortalitate Platonem," T p. 159). She reminds them of their earlier studies together in which she had surpassed both of them while they, especially Orestes, had been a laughingstock to others (60).

The venom was evidently spent here, for in the letter to Frontonus Carito, dated the same day as the invective, there is reasoned argument rather than vilification. The charges against her, she believes, must be based solely on envy, for they have no basis in fact inasmuch "as I am now absent from my father in time and place" ("Interea nanque dum longius, atque diutius, a Patre absum," T p. 112). However, she considers it a great honor that she has been compared with her father, who is such a good orator. "I am very grateful, therefore," she concludes her letter, "to each of my two detractors and not less to him who exalts the father's greater knowledge rather than strains to demonstrate the lack of learning of an ignorant daughter" ("Multas igitur utrique delatori gratias habeo, neque inferiores illi, qui scientiorem Patrem extollit, quam qui imperitae filiae nititur dediscenda monstrare," T p. 113).

About Gismunda's (Cassandra's) charge she writes to Lorenzo Capreolo (Boniface Bembo): "(If I may say so), let no one of the learned be unaware of my talent" ("Meum (si dici licet) nemo litteratorum nesciat ingenium," T p. 120). She expresses amazement that people of the same sex and age as herself, without any evidence other than hearsay, should believe such charges, since they are themselves learned and know that what she has done is not beyond probability. Moreover, she has praised both critics in the past (63; see the discussion there, preceding the summary, of the conflict in addressees of this letter).

A deeper prejudice underlies this charge that her father wrote her letters, namely, that a woman cannot be learned. Cereta wrote five letters in which she addressed the question of the relation between learning and sex (12, 54, 61, 71, and 77). Four of these are addressed to men, one to a woman.

Those addressed to learned men point out that there have been many learned women in the past and that this tradition has continued even to the present.[10] With remarkable insight she asserts that to single her out as a prodigy among women is really to show contempt for women in general in the form of condescension. At the same time, she admits that learned women are more rare than learned men and suggests that the reason for this state of affairs is that women have been conditioned to value their bodies more than their minds. She suggests also that women are weaker than men,[11] and that they need to be encouraged rather than opposed or falsely praised. But these differences are not decisive. A woman can be as learned as any man if she applies herself to that end. As she writes in one characteristic passage:

Those who aspire with greater integrity to virtue, in the beginning restrain the young soul and consider better things. They harden the body with sobriety and works, restrain their language, listen with their ears, place their talent in a state of wakefulness, arouse the mind to the contemplation of letters, always obedient to uprightness. For knowledge is not given as a gift but through energetic application. For the free mind, not shirking effort, always rises up more keenly to the good. And their desire to know grows ever more widely and deeply. Therefore, it is not because of some special holiness that we have been given by God the giver the gift of a more remarkable talent. Nature has sufficiently given its gifts to all. It has opened the doors of choice to all, through which reason sends envoys to the will from which they may bring back their desires with them.

At illae, quibus ad virtutem integritas maior aspirat, frenant principio iuvenilem animum, meditantur meliora consilia, durant sobrietate et laboribus corpus, cohibent deinde linguam, observant aures, componunt in vigilias ingenium, et mentem excitant in contemplationem ad literas probitati semper obnoxias. Neque enim datur dono scientia, sed studio. Nam liber animus labori non cedens acrior semper surgit ad bonum: et excrescunt longius illi atque latius desideria discendi. Esto igitur, ex nulla nostri sanctitate non simus a datore Deo ullo munere electioris ingenii donate: Donavit satis omnes Natura dotibus suis: Omnibus optionis suae portas aperuit, per quas ad voluntatem mittit ratio legatos a qua secum sua desideria reportent (T pp. 192–93).

She makes the same point much more polemically in the one letter in this group addressed to a woman, entitled "Against Women who Disparage Learned Women" ("Contra Mulieres, mulieribus doctis detrahentes"). It is easier to forgive men their foolish opinions than it is to "bear the babbling and chattering women, glowing with drunkenness and wine, who do injury by their impudent words not only to our sex but even more to themselves" (". . .garrientes blaterantesque foeminas ferre, . . . quae temulentia vinoque flagrantes non sexui modo, sed sibi plerumque dictis petulantibus injuriantur," T pp. 122–23). The only reason one woman criticizes another is that her own mind is inactive and rusty. In such a condition herself, she cannot bear to hear another praised. Cereta's advice is simple: give up the endless search for pleasure, devote disciplined attention to study, and be led by this latter path to wisdom (T pp. 124–25).

The Correspondence with Brother Thomas and the End of Cereta's Life

The only person to whom Cereta wrote from whom we have responses is Brother Thomas of Milan. There are seven extant letters: three from Cereta, three to her, and one from Brother Thomas to her father, Silvester. Some of the letters are, in part, responses to others within this group, though there are apparent allusions to others which have not been preserved. The letters are important because they tell us something about the outcome of the controversies in which Cereta was engaged during the last year of her correspondence, and they provide significant clues about her state of mind as she completed her volume of letters, furnishing a basis for reflection on the course of her life subsequent to this period of letter writing.

The order of these letters is not difficult to establish. The first (49) was penned by Cereta shortly after the death of her husband. She refers to herself as "lately so saddened" by his death. The second (68) is from Brother Thomas to Silvester and is fully dated. The last five follow one another closely, from November 4, 1487 to February 4, 1488.

Brother Thomas is unknown to me from sources other than these letters. He is not included in reference books on ecclesiastical writers. A Dominican friar from Milan, he represents himself to Silvester Cereta as one eager above all for learning. He was evidently trained in rhetoric, for he can appreciate the oratorical merits of several of Cereta's letters which he had received (IX: 57ff.). But he is above all concerned about sacred literature and laments the fact that today there are no Ambroses, Jeromes, or Augustines among us. He commends the works of these writers, saying that if we venerate them, we should read and imitate them. Cereta, in her letters, represents him as one brought up on the teachings of the philosophers (73; T p. 130). From these cursory statements we may conjecture that Brother Thomas possessed both a humanist and a scholastic education.

Tomasini maintains that he was Cereta's teacher, and in one place Cereta calls him such explicitly: "I for my part honor you my teacher" ("Ego enim Te praeceptorem meum veneror, . . ."

T p. 130). But this is not to be taken literally. In his letter to Silvester, Brother Thomas marvels at the letters of Laura that Silvester has sent to him and looks forward to receiving her entire volume of letters. These things he writes as if in surprise at her accomplishment (see IV: 115–19). Moreover, in a letter to Cereta he admits that his own learning is not equal to hers (XI: 253–54). And, in another response, he acknowledges that he lacks oratorical skill (XII: 53–63). Rather than her teacher, Cereta came to regard him as her spiritual counselor. He presents himself in all three of his letters to her as one giving advice, and she acknowledges in her final letter that she has taken his advice (78; T pp. 225, 226).

The thread that runs through their correspondence is provided in the first letter, written by Cereta only one or two months after the death of her husband. In it she refers to earlier letters of his, not extant, which accuse her of being filled with secular learning but showing nothing of Christian feeling in her writings, for which reason they appear dangerous to him (49; T p. 114). Cereta responds by declaring that she is neither an orator nor a theologian and that she does "not wish to struggle against God by contemplating something laborious, but to believe" ("Nolo in Deum laboriosum aliquid contemplando moliri, sed credere," T p. 114). It is in this letter that she renounces the brief and fallen glory of this life which separates us from true religion. She even asserts that monastic security is not unknown to her (doubtless a reference to the two years she spent in the monastery from the ages of seven to nine) and that sometimes she longs to have it renewed (ibid., pp. 116–17). The importance of these assertions in a letter to Brother Thomas derives from the later letters. Already in this letter, written one year prior to the other correspondence in this group, she shows herself susceptible to his judgments and inclined to regard him as a spiritual counselor.

The second letter in the series is that from Brother Thomas to Silvester in which, as we have seen, he praises Cereta and expresses surprise and admiration for her work. But the third letter, from Brother Thomas to Cereta herself, dated less than one month later (November 4, 1487), is filled with criticism. Cereta, attacked by her critics, had also apparently come to believe that Brother Thomas had criticized her and she had written him a letter, no longer extant, in which she had spoken to him in the sharpest language, perhaps attacking both his philosophical and his oratorical ability. (See his response, below, x, *passim.*) He accuses her of having listened to false reports and says that she has destroyed his predisposition to view her favorably. He does not like her oratorical incense. He advises her to "smooth your forehead, cut off the sting of your tongue, blunt your pen, beloved sister, and moderate your conduct with a file" (v: 92–93).

The next letter is from Cereta, dated seven days after this letter from Brother Thomas. Her letter begins in a belligerent tone, expressing anger at his criticisms of her and insisting on her religious sincerity. Her response does not raise the question of the relation of her learning to her piety – suggesting the absence of conflict between the two in her mind – but only affirms the strength of her devotion to religion. The force with which she does so indicates that this was a vulnerable point in her armor. It is perhaps for this reason that the letter ends by being deferential.

Two weeks later (November 25, 1487) Brother Thomas responded to Cereta's letter of November 11. He criticizes her once again for her attacks on others, especially on people unworthy of her in the first place, and denies that he has ever attacked or denounced her. Her behavior, however, has led him to reflect on what its basic cause might be. He suggests that it lies in the rhetorical ideal adopted by Cereta. The orator seeks to exalt himself and sway a crowd. He is not interested in truth. Cereta has too great a commitment to this ideal, and he begs her to give it up in favor of the Christian ideal of love, which is patient and supportive and rejoices in the truth.

This is the central theme of Brother Thomas's last letter, dated December 12, 1487, just over two weeks after the preceding one. It is unclear whether Cereta has written in between. If she did she was critical, to judge by what Brother Thomas says in this letter. He tells her that she is full of rhetoric, that is, feelings that are out of control, impatience, and ambition. But true humanity lies elsewhere, in gentleness, patience, and humility. These she should cultivate, keeping in mind always the thought of death.

Brother Thomas in these last letters has made it clear that religious humility is more to be desired than learning and that the rhetorical ideal in particular should be set aside in favor of a contrite religious consciousness. This was apparently the advice he had given Cereta much earlier, as suggested in her first letter to him. How did she respond this time?

It may be that the response we have is the only other letter Cereta wrote to Brother Thomas (78). She begins this letter by saying that she wishes to respond to one and another of his letters. Contrary to what his letters indicated that she had said about him in the past, here she is profuse with her praise of his learning and skill, both in thought and in writing. She marvels at his eloquence and polished style and at his knowledge of philosophy and theology. Moreover, she commends his monastic discipline by which he hastens to God and regards this world as transitory, not seeking its fame. In this connection, she also acknowledges the desert fathers and the purity they found in their cloistered cells, though she adds (upholding the "active" life) that others entered the cities and proclaimed the gospel there. It is evident here that her attitude has changed from one of criticism to one of deference.

Two things, she concludes, she has learned from him. First, this body is a vain and fallacious token of the soul, and the conscience is much the more precious. For this reason, she writes, "I have ceased to trust in the bright glory of humane letters, lest by chance a mind deprived by vanity and an unwise concern for the future should unhappily seek the happiness of a transitory name" ("retraxi ab illustri humanorum litterarum gloria consilium ne forte vanitate mens orba et imprudens diligentia futuri foelicitatem caduci nominis quaerat infelix," T p. 225). Further on she adds: "We ought not to let our zeal for knowledge possess us, as if we were born for letters alone" ("non debet plus vigiliae restare semper nobis in studio, tamquam simus solis litteris natae," ibid.). This leads to the second lesson he has taught her: "Thus I have determined to place myself in your hands for guidance toward a surer way" ("Sic tui exemplo, ad regimen securioris viae, porrigere tuas in manus institui," ibid., p. 226). And, she adds:

> I should thank you even more, because through quiet urging you have released me from this burden of writing, pitying perhaps my many errors. Closed, therefore, too, is this first part of my familiar letters, choked by a bloodless style, disorderly, and summarily and cursorily recounted.
>
> (Hinc cumulatiores tibi debeo gratias, quod sub tacito hortatu levaveris me hoc scribendi ponduscuIo, numerosi erroris forte misertus. Clauditur ergo familiarium Epistolarum hic prima pars sub delumbi, et ab ordine in diversum abducto stilo strictim, capitulatimque comprehensa. Ibid.)

In the concluding paragraph of this letter, Cereta does not say she will write no longer. But she does say that she will turn her attention now to higher things. This could mean the practice of religious devotion or it could mean the study of sacred literature. Whatever the case, it is interesting that she connects this higher activity with leisure, suggesting that she has come to the end of her earlier strenuous preoccupations, i.e., her activity as a humanist. It seems that, swayed finally by the admonitions of Brother Thomas, she abandons her own earlier self-confident attitude as a humanist intellectual and becomes a different kind of person.

Assessment of Conflicting Evidence

The conclusions reached in the preceding two sections do not correspond with one another. Analysis of Cereta's responses to critics, together with her epilogue and prologue, suggest a strong sense of herself as a female humanist intellectual. The correspondence with Brother Thomas, on the other hand, written after the responses to her critics but before her epilogue and prologue, suggest that she is renouncing her humanist studies. How are we to reconcile these two opposing tendencies?

In the few letters she wrote after her correspondence with Brother Thomas the conclusions reached in that correspondence appear to be borne out. In a letter written just one week after her last to Brother Thomas (79), she cites examples from both Christian and classical traditions to show that people have struggled against adversity, even as she considers that she has been doing through her studies. At this point in the letter she describes the place she has reached in her pilgrimage. She writes:

> For this reason, since some sadness always brands us, since there are no limits to miseries on the earth, and since our mind, struck by continual fear of the future, has nothing to hope for except God, I have devoted my efforts to universal rather than to human things. For virtue and knowledge grow together at the same pace as do the traveler and the road he travels. Therefore, the natural vigor of a loftier inclination grows within me, which changes the splendor of eloquence into

the most chaste opinions. Thus love, whose invincible strength vanquishes all things, increasing daily, summons me to an inner apprehension of sacred law.

(Quare quum aliquis nos semper dolor inurat, quum nullus si miseriarum modus in terris, et nihil habeat, praeter Deum, quod speret noster animus, continua futuri suspitione percussus, non tardavit me difficultas ulla consilii, quin generosum ex humanis ad catholica studium abducerem. Eo namque gradu congermanescunt virtus et scientia, quo viator et via. Crevit ergo majoris ingenii vivacitas, quae in castissimas sententias commutaret candorem eloquii: Sic ad interiorem sacrae legis agnitionem grandescens in dies me amor invitat: cuius invictae vires omnia devincunt, T p. 198).

The reference is explicit: she is giving up splendid eloquence for pure truth. Recognition of the sacred law (Scripture?) is daily vanquishing every other preoccupation.

This same frame of mind is evident in her "Warning against Avarice" (T 67, p. 199: "In Avaritiam Admonitio"), in which she argues that avarice is a reflection of too much concern for the present world. All riches will perish as the fates of the richest men in history have proved. One should look rather to eternity than to riches on earth (82). This sentiment reflects almost exactly the conclusions reached in the correspondence with Brother Thomas.

There is one other letter to be considered, addressed to Solitaria Europa and recalling her from the delights of a solitary life (81). Pagans, she tells her friend, retreated from the world because the only peace they hoped to find was in the world. But Christians hope for eternal peace and should not, therefore, seek to escape the entanglements in which every life is wrapped. She urges Europa to serve widows and young bereaved persons, so that as she grows older and approaches death there will be less bitterness in her heart. Note that Cereta is not calling Europa back to study but to some form of social service. The absence of any explicit reference to intellectual activity can be taken as evidence of a change in her attitude, for we can assume, since she wrote to her friend in Latin, that the recipient was a learned woman. At the same time, it is significant that Cereta does not counsel retreat. This suggests that she herself was not temperamentally predisposed to it but rather to some form of active domestic life.

In addition to these letters, there is the information provided by Trochismo that her portrait was preserved both by the Convent of the Minor Brothers of San Francesco di Paolo, whose suburban church she attended outside the Porta di Torrelunga of Brescia, and also by the Benedictine monks of S. Eufemia.[12] This supports the idea that she put a good deal of energy into religious devotion in her later years.

On the other side, in addition to her epilogue and prologue, there is her assertion, in the last letter to Brother Thomas as well as in her prologue, that these letters constitute the "first part" of her letters, suggesting that another part would follow. This would surely mean that she intended to continue writing letters. She may indeed have done so, and the letters may have perished because they were never officially published. But we have no evidence to support this conjecture.

There is, further, the suggestion of her brother Daniel, in his poem in praise of Brescia, that his sister Laura began to write poetry but that she died before she was able to get very far. But since we have no poem from her pen (see below, IX, the discussion of the one poem in her corpus) we cannot confirm Daniel's assertion. I do not believe that she wrote poems during the years of her humanist study, or some would probably have been included with her letters. If she wrote them, they were written later, during the eleven years of silence. If so, they must have suffered the same fate as any letters written during these later years: they perished because they were not published.

Finally, there is the tradition begun, it seems, by Ottavio Rossi, that she expounded philosophical theses publicly at the age of eighteen (i.e., at the time when her letters were brought to a conclusion) and that for seven years after she was twenty she taught publicly in Brescia. Although this has been repeated even up to the present day, it is nowhere attested in a primary source. I have been unable to locate evidence in the *Provisioni* for the city of Brescia during these years. This does not necessarily mean that the tradition is false, since she might have taught or lectured informally without the necessity of a provision to that effect. But there is no concrete evidence that she did undertake such teaching. The idea that she did this could support either the conclusion that she maintained her humanism or the conclusion that she turned away from it in favor of philosophy and theology.

The evidence that we have from the available sources does not allow us to reach a definitive conclusion. I would like to suggest one, however. Cereta was not turned away from her humanist studies because she came to prefer something else, but because as a woman she did not find any support in the intellectual world about her for the continued pursuit of her work.[13] In my judgment the decisive event in putting the lid on her humanist activities was the death of her father late in 1488, that is, six months or so after she published her collected letters. He had been her teacher and the strongest male supporter of her work; she had appealed to him when critics began to carp at her. Without father or husband, weary of the strife in which her humanist studies were lately involving her, she decided to seek more acceptable ways to live in society, and she turned her energies to religious studies or simply to an active domestic life informed by a deep piety. I would suggest further that having renounced "the wonderful example of Petrarch" and having turned toward a lifestyle more acceptable to those about her than that of a humanist intellectual, she gave up her vocation as a writer and disappeared from our view.

Cereta's Place in Quattrocento Humanism

As a minor figure in Quattrocento humanism and one not allowed to participate fully in the movement because of her sex, Cereta is all the more interesting in illustrating the diffusion of humanism among the upper classes in Italy's urban centers. What we see of her is a snapshot rather than a full portrait, for the materials we have from her pen were written over a relatively brief span of time, and the development we might have seen in her had she continued to publish what she wrote is not visible. Even so, the snapshot we have reveals some interesting conclusions.

Cereta was so caught up in the language and attitudes of Roman classical literature that the word "virtue" takes on for her its classical significations of honor, moral uprightness, achievement through discipline. The idea, however, is devoid of the largely social meaning it had in classical Rome (epitomized especially in the related notion of "duty"). For Cereta, the idea is most closely related to Petrarch and his search for fame through his writings. Cereta declares herself inspired by Petrarch's wonderful example. Her quest, like that of her mentor, becomes an individual pursuit. She, like him, would achieve eternal fame through her writing. We see in her, as in Petrarch, the rise of what Burckhardt called a new spirit of individualism, the birth of the self-conscious individual who wanted to be known for herself. That spirit must have been widely diffused in Italy from the time of Petrarch's death in 1374 until Cereta began to write just over one hundred years later. The very existence of her work and the attitude she expresses in it are a tribute to the new cultural direction Petrarch brought to European letters.

Common to the humanists was their belief that they had the power, through their pens, of making infamous or famous those whom they attacked or to whom they dedicated their translations, commentaries, and treatises. Cereta gave clear expression to this common belief. In both her epilogue and prologue and in at least one letter to Albert de Albertis she expresses her conviction that she is not only assuring the immortality of her own name, but also of the names of those whom she praises or to whom she dedicates her work or even to whom she simply writes.

Cereta reveals herself a humanist also in the form of her writings. Humanists were by and large writers of prose rather than of poetry, and in prose their favorite forms were letters, orations, and invectives. We have all three from Cereta. The most dominant literary form among the humanists was the epistle. All of them wrote letters and intended them in many cases for the public. The fact that Cereta composed her letters over such a brief span of time and did so with the intention of immortalizing her name clearly reveals that she not only wrote to individuals but intended her letters from the beginning as public documents. The fact that her father sent a number of her letters to Brother Thomas of Milan, who wrote back praising them, is a further indication of the same thing.

Some of Cereta's letters, as has been pointed out, are more or less formal orations, and, in addition, we have one oration written as such from her pen. These show that letters were often more than letters: they were occasions for formal presentations of an author's view on various subjects. The subjects of these formal letters—consolations on the death of a loved one, marriage, avarice, solitude, war—were favorite themes of many humanist writers.

Cereta also wrote an invective, another favorite form of humanist composition. She was perhaps familiar with the controversy between Poggio and Valla as well, perhaps, as with the less famous scrapes to which humanists were forever inclined. In any case, she was as wrathful and violent in her denunciations as Poggio, Valla, or Filelfo ever were.

In addition to the forms of humanist writing, Cereta also followed the humanists' interests in subject matter: biography, history and moral philosophy. Her autobiographical letter to Nazaria Olympia, her accounts of two conflicts in the territory around Brescia, and her discussion of Epicurus' philosophy on two occasions, as well as her constant references to "virtue," are illustrations of these interests.

On the other hand, she expresses no interest in speculative philosophy, dialectic, theology, law or medicine. Humanists in general were uninterested in these. So also is Cereta. It is characteristic of her that she says to Brother Thomas that she does not want to speculate but to believe. As noted earlier, although she mentions philosophers, she never discusses philosophical doctrines.

There is one exception to what has been said above: her interest in mathematics and astrology. She studied mathematics in order to understand the heavens, and she wanted to understand the heavens because she believed that they foretold the future. Even before she turned away completely from such preoccupations after the death of her husband, however, she had abandoned them in part to follow Petrarch. Moreover, she admitted that what can be known by this method is partial since all the data are never at hand or completely accurate. She was never without the humanists' awareness of the limitations on what one can know, so prominent a feature in Petrarch and in all who followed his interest in moral, rather than speculative, philosophy.

One of Cereta's letters, that to her sister Deodota, appears to follow self-consciously two humanist models: Petrarch's account of his ascent of Mont Ventoux and Valla's treatise *On Pleasure*. Her account of the journey moves on two levels at once: that of the mind or soul and that of the body. The spiritual journey invigorates the soul while the physical journey invigorates the body. It is, of course, the spiritual journey on which she enjoins her sister to keep her eyes focused. The analogy is not exact but is close to Petrarch's *Ascent of Mont Ventoux*. For Petrarch also the journey is both of soul and body. The bodily journey ends in fatigue and loss of way, the spiritual journey in a new knowledge of self. We do not find the self-conscious spiritual anguish in Cereta that we find in Petrarch, whose soul was overcome when he reached the top of the mountain and read a passage from Augustine's *Confessions* which brought him to greater self-awareness. But the wonderful example of Petrarch is nonetheless in the background of this description.

The second half of the same letter describes Epicurus' notion of pleasure as tranquillity of mind rather than as license. In this respect, the Christian is the most Epicurean of all people, for tranquillity and peace are what the Christian seeks. Certainly, Valla's *On Pleasure* and perhaps, secondarily, Traversari's translation of Diogenes Laertius' life of Epicurus, stand behind Cereta's discussion.

Still further indication of Cereta's adherence to the humanist movement is the affirmation of the active life which her defense of Epicurus presupposes and which we find throughout her corpus. Her letter to Solitaria Europa, in which she counsels her friend to accept the life of the world as training for eternal life, is the best example. Even when she is agreeing with Brother Thomas that a Christian flees from the world (the very charge indicates that he believes she is too much a part of it), she responds that while many examples of this can be found in Christian history, so also can examples of people going into the cities to preach. Like all humanists, she is a layperson, and she has the sensibilities of a layperson. She expresses no hostility toward the religious, as do Poggio or Valla, but she is committed to the active life. Pressured near the end of her period of writing to give it up, she does so only in a qualified way, and in her prologue announces that she will never fully do so. She admires her sister who is a nun, but only once, in the depths of her despair after the death of her husband, does she express a desire to withdraw into a monastic life. She quickly recovers from this, however, and finds her solace in her own form of monastic discipline, study and writing.

These considerations bring us back to Cereta's classical conception of virtue and its relation to her Christianity. I suggested earlier that there was no self-conscious conflict between the two. That is true, however, only because in her published works we have a snapshot rather than a portrait. In most of her letters she speaks of attaining virtue and of being a Christian as if they were synonymous. But there is a suggestion in her last letters that the two are not the same. We find, for example, in her very last letters references to keeping her eyes focused on Jesus Christ her Savior, where we might have expected, in keeping with earlier letters, references to virtue. At the same time, references to keeping her eyes focused on virtue do not disappear even in the last letters. There is a similar progression in her relation to classical antiquity. In all her earlier letters her references are almost exclusively to classical pagan writers. In her later letters she begins to mention the names of Christian fathers (though significantly, in true humanist fashion, no scholastics) and in one letter says she is reading Augustine and Jerome. Even so, her specific references remain classical and pagan.

What this means, I believe, is that Cereta, even in the brief span of her published writings, was beginning to sense a tension between classical and Christian antiquity which, had she continued to write or publish, would have required deeper reflection and resolution. Certainly Brother Thomas believed that such a tension existed and that Cereta was more pagan than Christian in her sensibilities (his intuition was correct in the sense that her literary models were more pagan but certainly not in the sense that she lacked Christian piety). There is an interesting parallel in the work of Erasmus. In an *Oration on Peace and Discord* which he wrote as a young man of twenty-one (1488) while residing in a monastery, he speaks of peace or harmony as a virtue necessary for human happiness. But in his *Complaint of Peace* written twenty-nine years later (1517) it is the teachings of Christ which breathe peace and militate against war. Erasmus progresses from the classical pagan notion of "virtue" imbibed in his early preoccupation with classical Roman authors to the Christian notion of following the way of Christ. In moving from the first to the second he did not replace one with the other but integrated the pagan into the Christian frame of reference. Something of the same movement is beginning to happen in Cereta. We must remember, however, that what we have from her pen was written while she was between the ages of sixteen and eighteen. It is unfortunate that this subsequent process of the integration of the traditions of her youth was cut short.

Notes

1. The sources for these and other details of her biography will be presented below where her life is more closely analyzed. The extant sources will be referred to in the text and notes as T (Tomasini), Vt (Vatican MS), and Ve (Venice MS). For a description and analysis of these sources, and for a summary of all the extant materials, see Part Two. In the summary of extant materials, the items are placed in chronological order and so numbered from 1 to 84. Reference is often made to these summaries in the body of the essay.

2. The first mention of this fact, so far as I have been able to determine, is in Ottavio Rossi, *Elogi istorici de' Bresciani illustri* (Brescia: Bartolomeo Fontana, 1620), 200.

3. M. Helius Capriolus, *Chronica de rebus Brixianorum* (Brescia: Arundo Arondo, 1505), Book 13.

4. The first to do so was Tomasini (see Part Two), whose edition of her letters is preceded by a biography. The second was Giorando Trochismo, "Vita, costumi, e scritti di Laura Cereta Serina, nobile Bresciana," in the collection of Abbate Giambattista Rodella, *Le dame Bresciane per sapere, per costume, e per virtù eccellenti* (Brescia, 1789), manuscript di Rosa no. 15, Queriniana. Both are based on the letters in the Tomasini collection, even though Trochismo knew of other sources more complete than Tomasini's.

5. Trochismo lists nineteen sources, of which I have actually seen thirteen. In alphabetical order (with the dates of their writings when these are known to me) they are: Leandro Alberti, *Descrizione di tutta l'Italia* (1581); Marcello Alberti, *Istoria delle donne scienziate*; Bartolommeo Arnigio, *Le dieci veglie degli ammendata costumi dell'umana vita* (1577); Illuminato Calzavacca, *Universitas Heroum Brixiae* (1654); Elio Caprioli, *Chronica de rebus Brixianorum* (1505), Carlo Cartari, *Brixia erudita* (MS); Giambattista Chiaramonte, "Lettera premessa alle Notizie del P. Lana," *Nuova Raccolta d'Opuscoli scientifici e filologici* (Vol. 40, opus. 6, 1784); Francesco Agostino

della Chiesa, *Teatro delle donne Letterate*; Andrea Chiocco, "Lettera a Ottavio Rossi," in *Brescia* (1622); David Clement, *Bibliothèque curieuse*; Leonardo Cozzando, *Libreria Bresciana* (1685); Jacopo Gaddi, *De scriptoribus non ecclesiasticis* (1648); Ortensio Lando, *Forcianae Quaestiones* (1536); Michelangelo Mariani, *Istoria di Trento*; Angelo Maria Querini, Cardinal, *Specimen Brixianae Literaturae* (1739); Ottavio Rossi, *Elogi istorici di Bresciani illustri* (1620); Girolamo Tiraboschi, *Storia della letteratura italiana* (1823); Andrea Tiraqueau, *De legibus connubialibus* (1554); Jacopo Filippo Tomasini, "Prologue," to *Epistolae* (1640).

In the nineteenth century she is given a paragraph in Vincenzo Peroni, *Biblioteca Bresciana* (Brescia, 1816), 1:251–52.

Arnigio, Chiesa and M. Alberti maintain that she wrote poetry in Latin and/or the vernacular. But Tomasini, Trochismo, and Tiraboschi deny this. There is actually one poem, in Latin, in the extant collection of letters. It exists only in Vt and follows, as if appended to, letter 59, which was written by Brother Thomas of Milan to Silvester Cereta, her father. It is a letter in her praise and the poem, I believe, was also composed by Brother Thomas and is also (at least in part) in her praise. Probably the origin of the idea that she was a poet is her brother's eulogy of her after her death in his long poem *De foro et laudibus Brixiae* (IX) where he says: "The bordering country submitted to her tongue, a daughter so well known to the Pierian chorus [i.e., the Muses]." Then he adds: "Perhaps also she would have been received into that number, but a hostile fate prohibited more than a good beginning." ("Illi successit patria contermina linguae, Filia Pierio tam bene nota choro. Forsitan et numero suscepta fuisset in illo, Sed vetuit coeptis sors inimica piis.") The poem was published in Brescia by Gianmaria Mazzuchelli in 1778. I own a xerox copy of this edition.

Ottavio Rossi maintains that she defended theses in philosophy publicly at the age of eighteen and taught philosophy publicly for seven years from the age of twenty. Tomasini, Calzavacca, Cozzando, and Chiaramonte repeat this assertion. The earliest reference to her as a philosopher in these sources is Lando, who simply says "I will record now the female philosophers," then lists "Laura bresciana" as among them. Arnigio asserts that she was learned in astronomical and divine things and in moral philosophy.

The earliest reference to her following her death is that of Elio Caprioli who simply says that she wrote a volume of the most elegant epistles worthy of any man, and that she, though only a woman, surpassed many men in dignity and honor. Most writers either quote Caprioli or refer to his assertion. Those writings after 1640 also generally mention the letters published by Tomasini.

One writer, Tiraqueau, says that she wrote elegant letters to Savonarola, then of Ferrara. There is, however, no corroboration for this in the extant materials. At least one later writer mentions it, probably on the authority of Tiraqueau: Lucretia Marinella, *La Nobilta e l'eccellenza delle donne co'diffetti e marcamerti degli huomini* (Venice, 1621), p. 54: "Una nobile Bresciana detta Laura scrisse molte elegante Epistole a Frate Girolamo Savonarola" ("A noble Brescian named Laura wrote many elegant letters to Brother Girolamo Savonarola"). Cereta in this source is being cited as an example of a woman devoted to learning ("donne scientale, e di molte asti ornate" ibid., 51). The first edition of this work appeared in 1600. (I am indebted for this reference to Dr. Patricia H. Labalme.) Savonarola did come to preach in Brescia during the period when Cereta was actively writing, in 1486 and again in 1489. See P. Guerrini, "Fra Girolamo Savonarola predicatore a Brescia," *Brixia Sacra*, 6 (1916):213–18.

6. Pia Sartori Treves, *Una umanista Bresciana del secolo XV* (Brescia: F. Apollonio, 1904), 17 pp. (reprinted in *Illustrazione Bresciana*, 1 agosto, 1910, 7–10); Agostino Zanelli, "Laura Cereto," *Illustrazione Bresciana*, 9 aprile, 1905, 3–4; and Agostino Zanelli, "Laura Cereto al Vescovo Zane," *Brixia Sacra*, 14 (1923):173–78.

7. *Storia di Brescia: 2: La Dominazione Veneta (1426–1575)*, promossa e diretta da Giovanni Treccani degli Alfieri (Brescia: Morcelliana, 1963), *passim*, and especially 494–96, 546, 566. On p. 495 the date of her birth is given as 1496, a typographical error. She is said to be the oldest of seven children, rather than six. On p. 546 it is stated that Pilado (Gianfrancesco Boccardi) is praised by Laura Cereta. It was rather by Daniel Cereta in *De foro et laudibus Brixiae* that he was praised. On p. 566, n.1, the assertion that she taught philosophy at the age of twenty is repeated, but no source for the assertion is offered. In n. 2 it is said that about eighty letters were published by Tomasini, when in fact there were seventy-one; the same note also says that the Vatican codex contains seven of her letters, when in fact it contains eighty-four items.

8. See *Storia di Brescia*, 2, pp. 497–512. On the "German War" see the first paragraph of Appendix 2.

9. Aloysii Mundellae, *Dialogi medicinales decem* (Tiguri: Apud Froschoverum, 1555), Dialogue 7, f. 82r-82v, mentions the names Martinus Agathius, Daniel Carretus and his sister Laura, Nicolaus Siccus, Dominicus Mantua, Vincentius Canthus, M. Aurelius Francius, Andreas Callepius, Franciscus Quintianus and his brother Coelius, and Octavius Pater as among those who were participants in discussions in his home. The passage including Laura's name reads: "Quibus quoque accedit Daniel Carretus noster modestia primum clarus, necnon medicinae atque poetices scientia excellentissimus, Lauraque illius familiae foemina pudicissima, et castissima. . . ." Laura never mentions Mondella or any of these participants in her letters, nor does her brother Daniel in his poem in praise of Brescia, which cites many outstanding citizens.

Peroni says of Mondella that he was a doctor learned in Latin,

Greek, Hebrew and Arabic, and that he had much erudition in botany. He was among the first to base his practice of medicine on the actual study of the human body. He died, ca. 1530. (*Biblioteca Bresciana*, Vol. 2, 282–83)

10. She mentions three of her contemporaries. Of these, Cassandra Fedele and Isotta Nogarola are well-known (see 55 on Cassandra; see below, n. 11 on Isotta). The third, Niculosa, is Nicolosia Sanuta, for whom two writings are listed in the *Iter Italicum*, a letter in the archives of Mantua and a speech to Bessarion in Bologna (*ut matronis ornamenta restituantur*). But in Ottob. lat. 1196 (*Iter Italicum*, 2, 428) it is said that the speech was composed for her by Filelfo.

11. This may well be a reference to Isotta Nogarola's letters and subsequent dialogue on the relative guilt of Adam and Eve, published in the 1450s. Isotta had argued that Eve was weaker than Adam and could not be held responsible for universal sin. On her works and the literature about her, see Margaret King, "The Religious Retreat of Isotta Nogarola," *Signs* 3 (1978), and "Thwarted Ambitions: Six Learned Women of the Italian Renaissance," *Soundings* 59 (1976):283–89, 301–2.

12. Trochismo, "Vita, costumi e scritti di Laura Cereta Serina nobile Bresciana," p. 43.

13. Margaret King has reached this same conclusion in her study of a number of women humanists. See "Thwarted Ambitions" (n. 11 above) and "Book-Lined Cells: Women and Humanism in the Early Italian Renaissance," in Patricia H. Labalme, ed., *Beyond their Sex: Learned Women of the European Past* (New York: New York University Press, 1980), pp.66–90.

PART TWO

Analysis of the Sources and the Nature of Extant Materials

Nature of Extant Materials

Four copies of the letters and orations of Laura Cereta are known to me to have existed in manuscript. A description of each follows.

1. [T] One, no longer extant, belonged to Ottavio Rossi, who published a brief life of Cereta in 1620, together with two of her letters. He was the first to mention that she taught philosophy publicly for seven years after reaching the age of twenty. Phillip Jacob Tomasini borrowed the Rossi manuscript and published its contents in 1640: *Laurae Ceretae Brixiensis Feminae Clarissimae Epistolae jam primum e M S in lucem productae* (Padua: Sebastiano Sardi, 1640). In 1636 Tomasini had published the letters and orations of Cassandra Fedele. These two are bound together in the Biblioteca Riccardiana in Florence, though not in the Biblioteca Marucelliana in Florence, which also has a copy. I own both a xerox and a microfilm copy of this edition. It is the text consistently referred to in this book because it is the most available source. It contains seventy-one letters. The letters are numbered and the numbering actually goes to 72, not including the prologue (+ 1) which is unnumbered at the beginning. However, there are no letters numbered 19, 20, or 51 (-3) and two letters are numbered 47 (+ 1) (The numbering goes 47, 48, 47, 49). Thus 72 + 1 − 3 + 1 = 71.

2. [Vt] the Vatican manuscript (Vat. lat. 3176. cart. 3. XVI in 73 fols.) is written in a cursive script. The hand is similar throughout, although the lines are closer together after the first few folios. Sometimes corrections are made in the margins by the same hand, and for the first few folios words are written in the margins which appear exactly the same in the text. Abbreviations are not uniform throughout. For example, *vel* is sometimes written out, sometimes abbreviated. The same is true of some other abbreviations. The text is preceded by a table of contents numbering each of eighty-three items that appear in it (a poem at the end of Vt 59 is unnumbered: see below, letter IX) and listing the correspondents to whom each letter is addressed. Each item is also numbered in the text.

I have studied Vt at the Vatican Library, especially the watermarks, in order to determine as closely as possible the date of its composition, but the watermarks were not clearly enough definable for me to make that determination.

I own a microfilm copy of this manuscript.

3. [Ve] The Venice manuscript (Marc. cod. Lat., XI, 28 [4186]mbr. XV, 154 fols.) is written in the humanist hand developed by Poggio. The lines are very short, containing only four or five words each, and although this leaves wide margins, there are no words written in the margins. Each letter begins with a large decorative capital letter with a flowery design. None of the letters is numbered.

The manuscript presents several problems. Unfortunately, I have not been able to study the manuscript at first hand but only a microfilm copy of it which I obtained from the Biblioteca Marciana.

First, the manuscript as we now have it begins on folio 11. According to the index at the end of the manuscript, the prologue dedicating the work to Cardinal Ascanius Maria Sforza filled the first six of these folios and the mock funeral oration for an ass began on folio 7.

Second, folio 49 verso begins with a letter to Laura's father, Silvester, (Vt 27, T 18), but 50 recto takes up a letter to Felix Tadinus (Vt 32, T 25). The scribe omitted about half the letter to Silvester and copied instead the first few lines of a letter to Felix Tadinus. In Vt and T there are six letters in between these letters to Silvester and Tadino. Why the intervening letters were omitted and why these two were each copied only in part is a mystery.

If we count all the items contained in whole or in part in Ve the number comes to seventy-four. Only seventy-one items, however, are contained in their complete form.

4. [Z] A fourth MS belonged to D. Baldassare Zamboni and, so far as I know, is no longer extant. Trochismo, who mentions it in his life of Cereta written in 1789, says that it contained eleven items not in the Rossi MS (T), in addition to the funeral oration. Assuming that it also contained all the items in the Rossi MS, this would make it almost as complete as Vt, which contains thirteen items not in Rossi (T).

Although Vt contains all the materials in the other extant sources, it does not agree with them in all respects, nor does it have the appearance of a formal copy (Ve is much more carefully written and decorated). Thus it was probably not the archetype from which the others were copied. Based on information now available, the most plausible hypothesis is that each of these copies was made from an archetype. Thus:

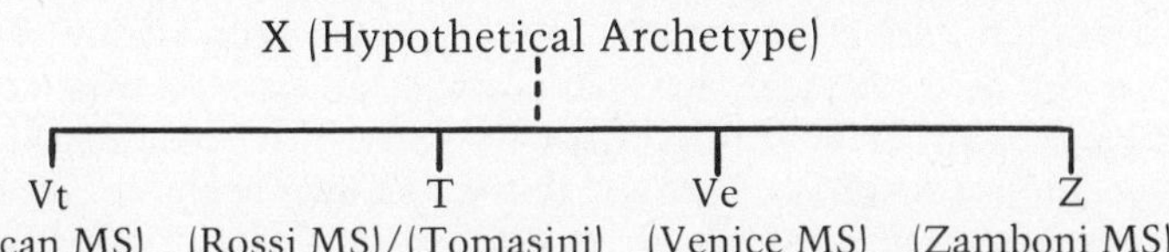

The Vatican MS with eighty-three items contains everything extant from Cereta's pen. The Vatican MS and Ve share seven letters missing in T, but T and Vt have in common five letters missing in Ve. Further, Vt contains four letters and a poem which none of the other sources contains, all written by Brother Thomas, three to Cereta and one to her father, Silvester. One other item, the funeral oration, is contained only in part in Ve.

With two exceptions (excepting also the scribal errors and the lacunae in Ve) the letters as contained in each of the extant sources are identical. Tomasini 28 (Vt 35, Ve 30), omits several lines at the beginning which are contained in both the other sources. So also does T 64 (Vt 76, Ve 66). There are a few minor differences in connectives, but these are negligible.

There are four cases of discrepancies in the dating of letters. In three of these, where the letters appear in all the extant sources, T and Ve agree (Vt 60, 64, 72; T 52, 71, 60; Ve 54, 73, 62). In the fourth case, the letter is only extant in T (23) and Vt (30).

There are two differences in the addressees of letters. Tomasini 12 is addressed to Angelo Capello, but the same letter is addressed in Vt 21 and Ve 20 to John Olivieri, the grammarian. In the second case, Ve 55 and T 53 are addressed to Lorenzo Capreolo, while Vt 66 (the same letter) is addressed to Boniface Bembo. (For a discussion of this discrepancy, see below, 63.)

Of the eighty-four extant items, seventy-eight are letters written by Cereta to fifty different correspondents, four are letters written by Brother Thomas, one is a poem probably also by Brother Thomas, and one is Cereta's mock funeral oration. Only twelve correspondents received more than one letter, and with only five is there anything approaching an extensive correspondence.

These five are Albert de Albertis (T 14, 22, 27, 29, 32, 41, 45, 55), Michael Baetus (T 21, 26, 36, Vt 7), John Olivieri (T 1, 12, 16, 33, 38, 39), Peter Serina (T 6, 8, 10, Vt 9), and Brother Thomas of Milan (T 52, 56, 71 to him, Vt 61, 63, 65 from him, and Vt 59 from him to Silvester, her father). Fourteen of the correspondents are women, none of whom receives more than one letter. Eleven of the letters are addressed to members of Cereta's family. The others are written to people of learning in various walks of life. Two were well-known prelates, Cardinal Ascanius Maria Sforza and Bishop Paul Zane of Brescia. Brother Thomas of Florence and Brother Ludovico de la Turre were venerated as preachers. Among the lawyers to whom she wrote were Sigismund de Buccis, Dominico Patusio, Francesco Prandono, and Albert de Albertis (whom she also speaks of as learned in philosophy). Michael Baetus and Raimondus Fortunatus were natural philosophers. Men trained in the humanist disciplines of grammar and rhetoric included Ludovico Cendrata, Francesco Fontana, Boniface Bembo and John Olivieri. Only a few of these rise above obscurity today. Those known to me from sources other than these letters are Cardinal Ascanius Maria Sforza, Bishop Paul Zane, Cassandra Fedele, Boniface Bembo, and Ludovico Cendrata. (Biographical data on these persons may be found below in 83, 19, 55, 10, and 35 respectively.)

Most of Cereta's letters are brief and untitled. Some, however, are lengthy. Among these, thirteen are more or less formal orations or discourses with titles, and a fourteenth, although untitled, can be regarded as a formal discourse. With some overlapping, these deal for the most part with themes characteristic of the humanist literature of her day. Two, for example, are on the instability of fate or fortune (51 and 56), two are on marriage (32 and 51), two are consolations in the face of the death of a loved one (52 and 67), one is an invective against two of her detractors (60), one is on avarice (82), one on the false delights of a solitary life (81), two on war (27 and 35), and one on the Eucharist (19). Perhaps the most original is one on her defense of the liberal instruction of women. Her positive attitude toward learned women and her aggressive defense of them may well be unique in the literature of the Quattrocento (78). The obverse of this is her invocation against women who waste their time on frivolous activity (54). Finally, her letter to Cassandra Fedele, which describes with much classical knowledge a voyage to the underworld, may be regarded, until its final paragraph, as a formal discourse (55).

Dating of Extant Materials

Except for T 1 (39), dated June 7, 1486, Cereta does not give the year for any of her letters, though with two exceptions (her funeral oration and the prologue to her letters) she always states the month and the day of the month. The letter of Brother Thomas to her father Silvester, Vt 59 (68), is dated October 9, 1487. Three other letters can be dated with certainty on the basis of evidence within the letters themselves. In T 44 (65) she discusses the "German War" of 1487. This war broke out in the spring after preparations in 1486. The Germans took Rovereto on May 10. The last battle of the war was at Calliano on August 10. The Germans (mysteriously according to Cereta) did not press their advantage but returned home. Peace was concluded on November 13, 1487. Cereta's letter is dated August 29, and therefore certainly was written in 1487. In T 55 (24) the position of the heavens described in great detail within the letter places it in 1485. In T 12 (38) the same kind of data places that letter in 1486.

Data which appear precise in a few other letters in reality are not. For example, in T 34 (33) she says that she has worked at her studies for seven years, but in T 46 (12) she says she began her studies when she was less than ten, while in T 59 (50) she says she began them at the age of eleven. In T 69 (35) she refers to the war with Ferrara, saying that we have now passed a more tranquil five years. That war broke out in 1480, ceased momentarily in 1482, then resumed the same year and concluded in 1484. It is impossible to determine from what point to measure the more tranquil five years. Again, Vt 8 (27) states that the Turks have penetrated into Apulia in southern Italy. This actually occurred in 1480, when Cereta was only eleven and could not yet have written this letter. She is therefore not writing about the penetration as a contemporary event, even though the letter gives this impression.

There is one central event in Cereta's life which enables us to date a number of other letters with precision. She was married when she had just turned fifteen to a local merchant, Peter Serina, who died after they had been married for only eighteen months. Thus they were married around December 1484 or January 1485, and he died near the end of July 1486 (the last letter to him is dated July 17, 1486 and the first letter mentioning his death August 5, 1486).

There are a number of letters written to him or referring to him as alive. Those which bear a month date of August, September, or October during his life must have been written in 1485, since she was married for only one passing of these months. Other letters can be dated around these (3, 11, 16, 17, 18, 29, and 44).

Immediately after he died, her grief was overwhelming and immediate. There are letters expressing an immediacy of grief which require a date of 1486 (46–49). There are other letters in which the grief is reflected, in which she is talking *about* how she felt immediately afterwards (rather than expressing contemporary feelings), letters that reveal a process of internalization of grief (50–57, 64, 67, and 79). In the letters written immediately after his death she expresses a longing to die herself, but in the later letters which speak about his death this longing has disappeared and has been replaced by a longing for God, a longing to see Peter in the next world, a longing for virtue, or a longing for studies.

In her autobiographical letter to Nazaria Olympia (50), she says that the death of her husband will always leave her sad and more or less miserable. Her later letters are more somber. Many deal with the themes of fate and fortune, marriage and death. They contrast with letters known to have been written prior to his death which reflect a happy state of mind, free from deep care or suffering. I have therefore placed earlier those letters which reflect this carefree state of mind (1, 7–9, 13, 25, 33, 37, 38, and 43).

Another change, related to this same situation, is Cereta's attitude toward astrology and the desire to know the heavens. Her one dated letter that precedes her husband's death is an elaborate description of the heavens. Tomasini 55 and 12 (24 and 38) which can be dated on the basis of the description of the heavens within them, also precede his death. Letters written after his death, on the other hand, especially those on fate and fortune, state that she has lost interest in this practice and, indeed, it ceases. Hence, I have dated all the letters containing such descriptions or expressing a desire to know the heavens prior to her husband's death. (In addition to those already mentioned, these include 2, 13, 32, 35, 42, and 43.)

With regard to letters written prior to her husband's death, T 34 (33) mentions T 5 (2). There are a number of letters written after her husband's death which refer to other letters and so help with the dating of letters relative to each other. Vatican 59 (68), which has a year date given, refers to the content of T 12, 31, 35, 55, and 57 (38, 54, 55, 24, and 21 respectively), all of which must therefore precede it. The same letter may also refer to T 69 (35). Vatican 59 and T 61 (68 and 60) precede Vt 63 (74) which mentions both. Indeed, the entire exchange with Brother Thomas is closely related to Vt 59 and can be dated in proximity to it. Vatican 66 (63) refers to T 35 (55) which must therefore precede it.

The controversies which occupied Cereta after her husband's death also aid us in dating letters. The envy against her had been aroused even prior to this time, partly on the basis of her public oration. But it increased when, after her husband's death, she threw herself into her studies and wrote even more (certainly longer) letters. Once she recovered from her grief, indeed, as part of the process of recovery Cereta wrote more and was less inclined to be silent in the face of criticism. The criticism was of two kinds: that her father authored her letters and (related to it) that women could not be learned. Letters dealing with these themes belong for the most part to 1487 (42, 53, 54, 59, 61, 63, 66, 67, 70, and 78).

A *terminus ad quem* for all the letters is established by the death of Cereta's father, Silvester, either late in 1488 or early in 1489. In a list of those eligible for public office, recorded in the *Provisioni* (f.104v) of the Brescian City Council on December 29, 1488, Silvester Cereta is listed, but as deceased. He may have been alive when the list was promulgated but then have died shortly afterwards. Or, he may have died just before the list was recorded. In any case, his name is missing from a similar list written on December 29, 1490 (f.104–5). Since many of the letters following her husband's death relate to the charge that her father wrote them, they presuppose that he is living. Moreover, given Cereta's close relationship to her father, his death would surely have been recorded by her in virtually any letter she might have penned after the fact.

Applying all these criteria, I have reached the conclusion that the eighty-four items handed down to us were written, in almost equal proportions (in terms of number but not in terms of length), during the twelve months prior to and the twenty months following her husband's death, that is, between July 1485 and March 1488. Thus she was almost sixteen when she began to write and only eighteen when she published her letters. This conclusion fits well with her statement in T p. 16 (Jan. 1, 1486), that already she has a large body of letters. It also corroborates her statement in her epilogue (T p. 228) that she is releasing her letters at a young age.

Table of Extant Materials

Following is a table of all the extant materials by and to Laura Cereta. The table has five columns. The first column gives the number of each item according to its chronological relationship to other items in the corpus. The second column gives the position each item occupies in each of the extant sources.. The third column gives the date of each item as found in Cereta, together with the year I have determined for the composition of each item. Except for letters 39 (Vt 10, T 1, Ve 9), and 68 (Vt 59), no years are given in the manuscripts. In the fourth column is the recipient of each letter in the Latin form given in Cereta. The final column contains the opening words of each letter.

Order	Vt	T	Ve	Date	Recipient	Incipit
84	1	Pro		no date (Mar. 1488)	ad D.D. Ascanium Mariam in titulum epistolarum prologus canio	Iejunum, et inexpertum adhuc
19	2		2	11 Kal. Oct. (Sept. 22, 1485)	Episcopum Brixiae, D.D. Paulum Zane	Catholica ecclesiae Romanae respublica rogatam
1	3		1	no date (1484 or 1485)	In Asinarum funus Oratio	Longlobati gregatim advenae
28	4		3	pridie Kal. Ian. (Dec. 31, 1485)	Felici Tadino, Physico	Naufragantis universi diluvium
4	5		4	13 Kal. Aug. (Jul. 20, 1485)	Benedicto Arsago, papiensi	Ingenii nostri primitiis
6	6		5	9 Kal. Aug. (Jul. 24, 1485)	Benedicto Arsago	Qui te erudiat Apollo,
42	7		6	Pridie Nonas Iulias (Jul. 6, 1486)	Michaeli Baeto, Clarensi Physico	Video in notatos
27	8		7	13 Kal. Ian. (Dec. 20, 1485)	Helenam Cesaream	Audisti? Iam fama crevit
11	9		8	Idibus Aug. (Aug. 13, 1485)	Petro Serinae viro	Ex litteris tuis
39	10	1	9	Septimo Idus Iunii, circa meridiem 1486 (June 7, 1486)	Ioanni Oliverio Grammatico	In huius horae discursu
29	11	2	10	Kal. Ian. (Jan. 1, 1486)	Sigismundo de Buccis, LL. Doct.	Quanquam in praeturam

Order	Vt	T	Ve	Date	Recipient	Incipit
10	12	3	11	Nonis Aug. (Aug. 5, 1485)	Bonifacio Bembo	Offendis titulos, Bembe,
16	13	4	12	Quarto idus Sept. (Sept. 10, 1485)	Dominico Patusio Legistae	Unas nuper a te litteras
2	14	5	13	Pridie Nonas Iul. (July 6, 1485)	Ludovico de Leno, Avunculo	Primior maternae stirpis
44	15	6	14	16 Kal. Aug. (July 17, 1486)	Petro Serinae Consorti	Funestam orbitatem tuam
18	16	7	15	Pridie Idus Sept. (Sept. 12, 1485)	Francisco Prandono I.C.	Petrum Serinam, virum
3	17	8	16	Pridie idus Iul. (July 14, 1485)	Petro Serinae	Agis me socordiae
17	18	9	17	Quarto Idus Sept. (Sept. 10, 1485)	Francisco Prandono I.C.	Instat nunc proximus
5	19	10	18	11 Kal. Aug. (July 22, 1485)	Petro Serinae viro suo	Dii meliores, quibus innocentiam
14	20	11	19	Nonis Sept. (Sept. 5, 1485)	Veronicae, Matri	Foelix nimium ad limitas
38	21	12	20	Nonis Iun. (June 5, 1486)	Angelo Capello (T); Io. Oliverio Grammatico (Vt & Ve)	Miraberis, certo scio
41	22	13	21	Kal. Iuliis (July 1, 1486)	Dianae Ceretae, soror	Heri et nudius tertius
22	23	14	22	Idibus Oct. (Oct. 15, 1485)	Alberto de Albertis I.C.	Suspicabar, et nunc auguror

Order	Vt	T	Ve	Date	Recipient	Incipit
20	24	15	23	Decimo Kal. Oct. (Sept. 23, 1485)	Petro Stellae	Iam medium abactae
40	25	16	24	Idibus Iuniis (June 13, 1486)	Io. Oliverio	Cleopatrae lautissimas coenas
23	26	17	25	Pridie Kal. Nov. (Oct. 31, 1485)	Clementi Longulo, Grammatico	Cato, et Socraticus
30	27	18	26	Kal. Feb. (Feb. 1, 1486)	Sylvestro Genitori	Vix recens commigraveram
26	28	21		Pridie Idus Dec. (Dec. 12, 1485)	Michaele Baeto Physico	Ego dudum abs te
31	29	22		Tertio nonas Feb. (Feb. 3, 1486)	Alberto de Albertis I.C.	Ego licet in hoc ocio
15	30	23		Nonis Feb. (Vt) (Feb. 5, 1486) Nonis Sept. (T) (Sept. 5, 1485)	Constantio Bonifacio	Alterna gratificandi vicissitudo
56	31	24		Idibus Aprilis (April 13, 1487)	Ad regium Oratorem Franciscum Fontanam Execratio contra Fortunam	Locavere majores nostri coelo
47	32	25	27	Quarto Idus Aug. (Aug. 10, 1486)	Felicem Tadinum	Solatrix mihi fuit
48	33	26	28	Idibus Aug. (Aug. 13, 1486)	Michaeli Carrariensi Physico	Legi litteras tuas

Order	Vt	T	Ve	Date	Recipient	Incipit
46	34	27	29	Nonis Aug. (Aug. 5, 1486)	Alberto de Albertis, Legistae	Magna et praeclara
57	35	28	30	Kal. Majis (May 1, 1487)	Felici Tadino Physico	Heu nascimur, serpunt* (T) Stellae et rerum eventus (Vt & Ve)
58	36	29	31	Nonis Majis (May 7, 1487)	Alberto de Albertis	Proposueram summo studio
53	37	30	32	Secundo nonas Feb. (Feb. 6, 1487)	Augustinum Aemilium deploratio	Voveram me templo Minervae
54	38	31	33	Pridie Idus Feb. (Feb. 12, 1487)	Augustinum Aemilium contra muliebram cultum Imprecatio	Ruru agabam solula
37	39	32	34	Nonis Majis (May 7, 1486)	Alberto de Albertis	Ibis nec poterit hinc
45	40	33	35	Kal. Aug. (Aug. 1, 1486)	Ioanni Oliverio	Gallus orator, immo Astrologus
33	41	34	36	Septimo Kal. Mar. (Feb. 26, 1486)	Bernardino de Leno, Consobrino	Satis ad Ludovicum avunculum
55	42	35	37	Idibus Aprilis (Apr. 13, 1487)	Cassandrae Venetae	Inter scientissimos poetas
43	43	36	38	8 Idus Iul. (July 8, 1486)	Michaeli Ba Physico	Arithmeticen, aut geometricen
66	44	37	39	Kal. Oct. (Oct. 1, 1487)	Clementi Longulo Grammatico	Studiosissimi litterarum

*There are four lines at the beginning of Vt and Ve missing in T, as follows: Stellae et rerum eventus indissolibilibus nodis astricti, fatale e sublimi in nos virus evibrant. Quo vel affligimur rapti, vel laqueis dirae mortis involvimur. Heu fata crudelia.

Order	Vt	T	Ve	Date	Recipient	Incipit
70	45	38	40	Pridie Kal. Nov. (Oct. 31, 1487)	Ioanni Oliverio	Ego quamquam non plena
7	46	39	41	Kal. Aug. (Aug. 1, 1485)	Io. Oliverio	Memini, neque oblivisci
9	47	40	42	Tertio Nonas Aug. (Aug. 3, 1485)	Hippolyto et Basilio	Multa licet, et quae
8	48	41	43	Kal. Sextilibus (Aug. 1, 1485)	Alberto de Albertis	Iunium Clarensis fori
13	49	42	44	Tertio Kal. Sept. (Aug. 29, 1485)	Fratri Thomae Florentino, Praedictaori	Sacrosanctae Virginis Matris
52	50	43	45	Pridie Kal. Dec. (Nov. 30, 1486)	Iulianum Trosculum Consolatoria de morte Filiolae	Hecubam nixus laboriosi
65	51	44	46	Tertio Kal. Sept. (Aug. 29, 1487)	Aloysio Dandolo Brixiae Quaestori de Theutonico conflistu	Criminantur multi Germanos
64	52	45	47	Nono Kal. Sept. (Aug. 23, 1487)	Alberto de Albertis	Videor satis suasa
12	53	46	48	Septimo Kal. Sept. (Aug. 25, 1485)	Fratri Ludovico de la Turre, Minorum Vicario	Ut mature nuper ex Urceis
34	54	47a	49	Decimo Kal. Mar. (Feb. 26, 1486)	Sanctae Pelegrinae	Eorum, qui de amicitia
62	55	48	50	Idibus Aug. (Aug. 13, 1487)	Venerandae Abbatissae S. Clarae	Quod ex ordine Ecclesiae
36	56	47b	51	Quarto Kal. Majas (Apr. 29, 1486)	Iacobo Basilisco	Perelegantes littere tuae

Order	Vt	T	Ve	Date	Recipient	Incipit
61	57	49	52	13 Kal. Aug. (July 20, 1487)	Alphonso Tiburtino	Litterae tue tametsi amici
59	58	50	53	Kal. Quintilibus (July 1, 1487)	Frontoni Carito	Quod scribis Eusebium
68	59			7 Idus Oct. 1487 (Oct. 9, 1487)	Silvestro Cereta frater Thomas Mediolanensis	Mirabar prodiga praecipitive quam
69	59 end			no date (probably same as 59)	probably Silvestro Cereta	Pascebat iam Phoẹbus equos
49	60	52	54	11 Kal. Nov. (Vt) (Oct. 21, 1486) Quarto Idus Sept. (T, Ve) (Sept. 10, 1486)	Fratri Thomae Mediolanensi	Ingenioli mei sententiolas exsucca
72	61			Pridie nonas Nov. (Nov. 4, 1487)	Laurae Ceretae Frater Thomas Mediolanensis	Operosa me desudatione melliflua satis
73	62	56	58	Tertio Idus Nov. (Nov. 11, 1487)	Fratri Thomae Mediolanensi	Iratius apum examen spinosior epistola
74	63			8 Kal. Dec. (Nov. 25, 1487)	Laurae Ceretae Frater Thomas Mediolanensis	Escandescentia mellicantium agmina
78	64	71	73	Pridie non. Feb. (Ve, T) (Feb. 4, 1488) 3 Id. Dec. (Vt) (Dec. 11, 1487)	Fratri Thomae de Mediolano	Responsura nunc unis atque alteris

Order	Vt	T	Ve	Date	Recipient	Incipit
75	65			Pridie Id. Dec. (Dec. 12, 1487)	Laurae Ceretae Frater Thomas Mediolanensis	Inflammavit ora vigentia aestuantenque
63	66	53	55	10 Kal. Sept. (Aug. 22, 1487)	Bonifacio Bembo (Vt) Laurentio Capreolo (Ve, T)	Accusat me nullo crimine
71	67	54	56	Kal. Nov. (Nov. 1, 1487)	Luciliam Vernaculam, contra Mulieres, mulieribus doctis detrahentes	Praecidendas in frustra linguas
24	68	55	57	Pridie Kal. Nov. (Oct. 31, 1485)	ad Albertum de Albertis De concurrentibus Coelestium Aspectuum ad Nativitatem hominum	Immensum Epistolae tuae mare
21	69	57	59	Id. Oct. (Oct. 15, 1486)	Regimundo Fortunato Physico, De influentiis Planetarum in vegetabilia	Aspectus et figurae coelestium
67	70	58	60	Octavo Idus Oct. (Oct. 8, 1486)	Martham Marcellani, de morte Mariti, Consolatoria	Optarem M. Crassum Parthieum
50	71	59	61	Nonis Nov. (Nov. 5, 1486)	Nazariam Olympicam de vita propria digesto	Sollicitata precibus tuis
51	72	60	62	12 Kal. Dec. (Vt) (Nov. 21, 1486) Septimo Kal. Dec. (T, Ve) (Nov. 26, 1486)	Barbaram Albertam de Instabilitate Fortuna et Gratulatorio de Nuptiis	Moderator honestatis nostrae Chrysippus
60	73	61	63	Kal. Quintilibus (July 1, 1487)	in Orestem et Phronicum Invectiva	Illiteratissimas litteras tuas

Order	Vt	T	Ve	Date	Recipient	Incipit
25	74	62	64	Quarto Idus Nov. (Nov. 10, 1485)	Constantio Bonifacio	Nuces hodie electissimus
76	75	63	65	pridie Idus Dec. (Dec. 12, 1487)	ad Sororem Deodatam Leonensem Monacham Totographia, Epicurique Defensio	Quaestiunculae tuae subtilitas ingenium
32	76	64	66	3 Nonas Feb. (Feb. 3, 1486)	Petrum Zenum Patavinum de Subeundo maritali iugo iudicum	Illigat se natali tuo exaltatum*
77	77	65	67	Idibus Jan. (Jan. 13, 1488)	in Bibulum Sempronium De liberale Mulierum institutione Defensio	Obverberant fatigatas aures tuae
79	78	66	68	Idibus Feb. (Feb. 13, 1488)	Bernardo Laurino Grammatico	Carminis et epistolae tuae erudita
82	79	67	69	Kal. Martiis (Mar. 1, 1487/8)	ad Lupum Cynicum in Avaritam Admonitio	Cynice, quid aurum sitiens
80	80	68	70	7 Kal. Martias (Feb. 26, 1487/8)	ad Marium Bonum, de Apparitione Phantasmatis	Inquieta et nugis incessabiliter

*Beginning with *exaltatum* a paragraph is omitted in T which is present in Vt and Ve, as follows: Illigat se natali tuo exaltatum in Piscium fatie secunda Veneris astrum. Cuius ascendentis imperium uxoriis tuis nexibus eblanditur, in domo bonae fortunae. Nam Venus et Pisces generationi disponunt. At nuptum alba tibi ex aspectu Jovis dabitur uxor, et ab ea videbis ex foelici filio nepotem. Horum influentiis discors accedit maior Arcturus, cuius octogemini radii tecum tunc coeperant sub caligine primae noctis oriri. Et quamquam in priore iugali promissu falli tibi stet casus, consolatior tamen postmodum adversus fortunam hostem evades. Et sub pudica lege coniugii fruiscentur se diu indissolubili nodo charitatis duo corda coniuncta.

Order	Vt	T	Ve	Date	Recipient	Incipit
35	81	69	71	Idibus Mar. (Mar. 15, 1486)	ad Ludovicum Cendratam Veronaeum, de Initiis et causis Militaribus, deque Bello Brixiano, et Coelestibus Prodigiis, Conquestio	Coelestiae Bellipotenti Numini Martis
81	82	70	72	4 Kal. Mar. (Feb. 29, 1487/8)	ad Solitariam Europam de falsa delectatione vitae privatae Admonitio	Quaesivi et percunctata sum vigiliore
83	83	72	74	Pridie Kal. Mar. (Feb. 28, 1488)	ad Rev. Sedis Apostolicae Card. D.D. Ascanium Mariam in Epistolas Epilogus	Rudis et intemperati calami nostri

Summary of the Content of Extant Materials

There are various ways in which the summaries of Cereta's writings could be organized. The most logical might appear to be to follow the order of the Vatican manuscript, since that source contains everything extant. Her intellectual development, however, can be made most visible to the reader through a chronological ordering of her writings, and this, it seems to me, is the most desirable alternative, especially since the materials are listed by order in each of the extant sources in the preceding section. In each of the sources the location and date of the letter will be provided, as well as a biographical sketch of each correspondent that is introduced, provided there is information available. In cases of unpublished correspondence, items will be listed as unedited, and the reader will be referred to Part Three of this study, where such letters, orations or poems are published for the first time.

1. Funeral Oration in Honor of Asellus

(1485, first half) Vt 3, Ve 1

For text, see below, I. Agostino Zanelli, a Brescian historian, professed an intention to edit the text of this oration, but he never did so. (See Agostino Zanelli, "Laura Cereto," *Illustrazione Bresciana*, 9 aprile, 1905, p. 4, n. 9). The oration carries no date and is impossible to locate precisely. But all the controversies in which Cereta engaged in 1486 and 1487 presuppose it, since the jealousy aroused by this oration was a principal cause of these controversies. Moreover, in her autobiographical statements she intimates that it was among the first of her productions. For these reasons, I believe it stands very near the beginning of Cereta's works. It was probably written during the first half of 1485.

Jacob Morelli, in his description of this oration in the Farsetti Library in Venice (*Della Biblioteca manoscritta di Tommaso Giuseppe Farsetti, Patrizio Veneto, e Baldassare del Sagr' Ordine gerusolimitan* [Venezia: Pietro Sarioni, 1780] par. 11, a car. 45, 46), states that it is a dialogue on death in which an afflicted father, Asinello, speaks and is then comforted by Cereta. Morelli was working with a source in which the first few pages of the oration were missing, and his description completely misses the point. The oration is in fact a mock encomium of an ass, not of a man. As a mock encomium the oration appears to be unique in the literature of the age. It seems to bear no direct resemblance to the works of Apuleius or Lucian on the subject of an ass.

There are three speakers. Soldus, the owner of the ass, laments his death. Philonacus, a slave born in the home of Soldus, is a shepherd who played and worked with the ass. Both Soldus and Philonacus express their grief, and Laura answers each in turn.

Summary. Cereta begins the discourse, expressing a desire to move the people present by speaking eloquently on this occasion. She raises the question of the immortality of the soul, pointing out that Theocritus, the Stoics, and the Peripatetics do not credit animals with immortality, a conclusion which should cause, not Soldus alone, but all of them to weep. She bids Soldus, an old man, to recite his poem of mourning; she in turn will sing of the heroes of the herd and mention the gods of the woods. [Many classical allusions are offered in embellishing this idea.] She laments the fact that butchers cut up donkeys' remains after they are dragged to a designated place with a rope; others remove their hooves; a pyre is built on which the beasts are burned. Why not, however, place them is compared with flowers on the riverbanks of Helicon and the meadows of Parnassus. You are hastening to fame, she concludes, on the horse of Bellerophon [Pegasus]. ❧

7. *To John Olivieri, Grammarian*
(August 1, 1485) Vt 46, T 39, Ve 41

This is the first of a number of letters addressed to John Olivieri, a grammarian (see below, 38, 39, 45, and 70). Olivieri was a well-known teacher in the province of Brescia during his day. Born around 1444 in Chiari, he completed his studies there and married Helena of an old Chiari family. He returned to Chiari to teach in 1487 after an absence of a few years and remained there until his death in 1497 (his wife died before him in 1493; Cereta mentions a significant visit from her, see below, 70). He taught a number of noblemen who in turn became men of learning, and he himself received a title of nobility before he died. He left no works. These and other details of his biography may be found in Ludovico Ricci, "Notizie di Giovanni Olivieri," *Nuova raccolta d'opuscoli scientifici e filologici* (Venezia: Simone Occhi, 1770), Vol. 20, opus. 6, pp. 3–18. In his discussion of some of Olivieri's pupils, Ricci does not mention the Cereta brothers commended to him by Cereta in this letter (Hippolytus and Basil) and in letter 39, below (Basil and Daniel). The letter fills almost two printed pages.

It is curious that Cereta rather than her father should have written this letter. Perhaps she was only assisting him in the matter or simply demonstrating to the future teacher of her brothers that there were already members in the Cereta household well educated in the disciplines he taught. Of course, the situation also reflects the fact that Olivieri's school was for boys only. Cereta could receive the kind of education Olivieri provided only if she could get it at home.

Summary. She sends greetings to his wife and thanks her for having been gracious to them before [indicating that this is not the beginning of a relationship between the two families]. She then commends to him two of her brothers, Hippolytus and Basil, as worthy pupils who need the instruction and discipline which a good teacher can provide. Their father, as well as th[e] rest of the family, hope that they will also enjoy their learni[ng] at his hands. She assures him that the boys will love him the more if he can instill in them a love for good litera[ture]. Success with them will redound to his own glory. ❧

in a tomb? Augustus and Julius, the dictators, had no more cause to place their beloved horses in a tomb. Did not the Romans order the crow to be honored with funeral rites because of its capacity to imitate the expression of the human voice?

Soldus then describes his ass, dearer to him than his own life. He bought the creature, of exquisite beauty, with a gold coin, and was almost immediately offered double the price in silver by someone else. Many times he rode on the animal's back. But who will carry him now in his old age? Must he walk on foot? He concludes with a lament on the miseries of old age.

Cereta responds that all grieve for the fate of Soldus. But Soldus' grief is excessive; nothing should cause a temperate man to lose his tranquillity of mind. The memory of the past should not torture him.

Soldus speaks again and describes the violent death of Asellus. While walking on a mountain, the ass slipped and fell down a steep ridge into a valley below where he was attacked by a wolf. How will Soldus and his family find protection now that Asellus is dead? Who will carry home the wood in the cold? Who will carry the crop of wheat?

Once again Cereta speaks, asserting that all share the fate of Asellus and that a sense of desperation is not the response called for. Otherwise, one will be destroyed by grief over, say, the loss of his children. Silence would be better.

Philonacus, a shepherd, makes his way through the throng of people to speak. He had been the keeper of Asellus and has many tales to tell of this ass's life. He describes how the animal learned to pull wagons and carriages so that he could pass through noisy crowds or bad weather without flinching. Unlike others of his species, he was not lazy, but could run with haste without having to be beaten. The stupid animal had a great knowledge of rainstorms, so that the position of his ears was a prophecy of their coming. He serenaded babies at their midday naps. He carried several people on his back when returning from the fields and never threw anyone off, though some fell now and then because of bad horsemanship. Once when he was punished with a beating for refusing to go into a river to wash off, he would not eat or rise for three days. On another occasion, when some boys tried to mount him, he kicked them. As punishment Philonacus tied him to a tree, exposing him to wild beasts. He became so cold and weak that it was only with difficulty that the next day he could be driven home with a cane. These and other incidents make Philonacus feel guilty about his treatment of Asellus. He weeps much more bitterly than Soldus, for he wants absolution. He asks Cereta to illuminate the suffering all this generates with the eloquence of a Demosthenes.

Cereta, in her peroration, also her longest single speech in the dialogue, says that she has spoken as eloquently as she could, though this may not always have proved efficacious, even as Cicero did not always win his cases. If what she has said has not thus far proved effective, all should remember that the soul is immortal. The deeds of Asellus will be remembered long after his death. Finally, both our happiness and our death come from the gods, a thought which should quiet us. Therefore, let reason be restored as ruler over our lives. Lay aside grief and take up the lyre. ❧

2. To Ludovico di Leno
(July 6, 1485) Vt 14, T 5, Ve 13

This is the only letter addressed to her maternal uncle, who is otherwise unknown to me. The di Leno family was long native to Brescia and numbered many among its noble citizens. The letter fills less than two printed pages.

Summary. The shield of the di Leno family contains a constellation of the heavens, the initial inspiration for Cereta's desire to learn astrology. Her study, however, has had as its purpose, not a reward from some Maecenas, but, following the wonderful example of Petrarch, her own eternal fame. For two other reasons also she studies: so that her mind might be possessed of the virtue of excellence and so that she might measure the distances to the stars. ❧

3. To Peter Serina, her husband
(July 14, 1485) Vt 17, T 8, Ve 16

Peter Serina was a local Brescian businessman to whom Cereta was married at the age of fifteen in December 1484 or January 1485. This is the first of four extant letters to him (for others, see below, 5, 11 and 44). Since she wrote to him in Latin, he must have had an education similar to hers, though as she hints in this letter, hers was better. Her letters were written to him while he was away on busir Venice and perhaps other cities. The couple were apparent a good deal even during their short marriage. He died fron after they had been married only eighteen months. Thi central one during the years her letters were composed, i chief factors enabling us to date the letters as precisely as letter fills just over one printed page.

Summary. Cereta expresses her anguish that her h not written her and wonders whether he is passing ment on her by his silence. She professes her whatever the charge. ❧

4. To Benedict Arsagus, Papiensi
(July 20, 1485) Vt 5, Ve 4

For text, see below, II. The recipient of this letter is unk from other sources.

Summary. No one should boast of wisdom but, im desire for immortality, of industriousness. She wri knowledge should be shared and because she seek talize her name. ❧

5. To Peter Serina, her husband
(July 22, 1485) Vt 19, T 10, Ve 18

On her husband; see above, 3.

Summary. Her husband chastised her for not writi when she did write, condemned her for speaking i She is distressed to the point of tears, even as she his departure for Venice. ❧

6. To Benedict Arsagus, Papiensi
(July 24, 1485) Vt 6, Ve 5

or text, see below, III. This is the second of two letter espondent (see above, 4).

ummary. She refers to one elegant letter written t rrespondent in both Greek and Latin. She attem eloquence with a rhetoric of her own in whic

8. *To Albert de Albertis*
(August 1, 1485) Vt 48, T 41, Ve 43

Albert de Albertis was a lawyer, who Vincenzo Peroni says left some manuscript works (*Biblioteca Bresciana*: Brescia, 1816, Vol. I, p. 20), although Mazzuchelli in *Gli Scrittori d'Italia*, I.1.297, regards Cereta's letters as the only source of knowledge about him. In addition to this letter see below, 22, 24, 31, 37, 46, 58, and 64. The letter fills about half a printed page.

Summary. She commends to him Junius of Clarensis, a secretary, and expresses her admiration for him. [She is apparently sending this as a letter of recommendation to gain a position for the young man.] ❧

9. *To Hippolytus and Basil, her brothers*
(August 3, 1485) Vt 47, T 40, Ve 42

This letter should be taken together with 7 above to the teacher to whom Cereta commended her two brothers. Here she addresses herself to her brothers and provides advice concerning their proper behavior as students. The letter fills about two printed pages.

Summary. Beyond what she has said to their teacher, she wants to exhort them to industry in learning. While others adorn themselves, tell jokes, or sleep, they should be watchful. For this purpose Olivieri is a distinguished teacher. If they will accept his counsel, they will gain a great deal of knowledge. They should also be mindful that they have a venerable heritage in their father, country, and customs, and should prove worthy of all this in their study. Either, she concludes, pleasure will separate you from great men or virtue from the dregs of the common crowd. The choice is yours. ❧

10. *To Boniface Bembo*
(August 5, 1485) Vt 12, T 3, Ve 11

Cereta wrote two letters to Boniface Bembo (for the other see below, 63). Bembo was born in Cremona, though the date of his birth is unknown. He first comes into the light in 1484 when he wrote a still unpublished *Oratio ad iuventutem Mediolanensem* while in Padua. He opened a private school in Paisola in 1487, but in 1489 was called to Pavia as a public lecturer. Around 1493 he was called to Rome by

Pope Innocent VIII to be professor of rhetoric. There he published a life of the Emperors Trajan and Nerva and translated some Greek fragments of Dio Cassius. Many of his orations and most of his poetry are lost. He died in Rome sometime after 1495, though the exact date is not known. See *Dizionario biographico degli Italiani* (Roma: Istituto della Enciclopedia Italiana), Vol. 8, 1966, pp. 111–12.

This letter fills about one printed page. It alludes to events or other letters which are not extant, so the context is not very clear. I would judge, however, that the allusions are to Cereta's father, Silvester.

Summary. She reproaches Bembo for representing himself as an insignificant person to her father, his patron. She assures him that his letters are dear to her father's heart, so much so that her father has endeared him to the rest of the family. Bembo's recent negative reaction to his friendship [the nature of which is not clear] has saddened him, though he remains constant in his affection. ❧

11. To Peter Serina

(August 13, 1485) Vt 9, Ve 8

For text, see below, IV. Her husband is presumably on the same business trip which brought forth letters 3 and 5 above.

Summary. She has read his letters carefully [none of them is extant] regarding the flood which has damaged his merchandise. She advises him to sell what is saleable before other merchants do the same, so that he can come out of the situation with as little financial damage as possible.

She then turns to another matter entirely. He had written her that she did not love him as much as she should. She is hurt by his accusation and does not know whether she should take it as a jest. What does he want from her? That she adorn her hair and paint her face? Unclaimed women act so. She would not want her husband at such a price. Her allegiance does not depend on such things. ❧

12. *To Brother Ludovico de la Turre*
(August 25, 1485) Vt 53, T 46, Ve 48

This is the only letter addressed to this preacher, who is unknown to me from other sources. It is extremely interesting from an autobiographical point of view. It fills two printed pages.

Summary. Returning recently from the convent of Chiara, Cereta was met by a young man who reported some gossip about her among the people who met there. Brother Ludovico was among those apparently surprised to find a young girl so well educated. But why should he be so surprised? In the first place, she is not distinguished in learning. But in the second place, it should be no more surprising that a woman is learned than that a man is. There have been learned women in the past, e.g., the Sibylline oracles and Sappho [see below, 77]. She is accustomed to the envy that lies behind some of the comments, for it has existed since she was ten years old. At that time she tore herself away from the common crowd and began to devote herself to study. She has progressed to the point that she believes her learning holds out the possibility of immortalizing her name. She desires this, she concludes, as much as you, a religious, desire through repentance to see the face of God.

13. *To Brother Thomas of Florence, Preacher*
(August 29, 1485) Vt 49, T 42, Ve 44

This is the only letter addressed to this preacher, who is unknown to me from other sources. Like the preceding letter, this one is extremely interesting. It reflects a rather clear difference between the recipient's religious preoccupations and Cereta's humanist attitude. The letter fills less than two printed pages.

Summary. In the sermon she heard him preach recently, he described the movement from the heavier to the lighter elements, the circles of the planets and fixed stars, and the nine hierarchies [presumably following Pseudo-Dionysius' Neoplatonic theory]. But as he preached, she thought of measuring the distance to the stars and planets, how far the planets are from each other and from us. Her purpose in thinking this way is to discern the will of God. For she believes that

God's will is rational and that it can be read in the heavens. He, however, has presented her with a problem, for in his sermon he said that we are not able to know the order which God gives to things. ❧

14. To Veronica, her mother

(September 5, 1485) Vt 20, T 11, Ve 19

This is the only letter to her mother who, according to this letter, did not live with Cereta. Cereta's role in the family is puzzling. We have already seen her commending her brothers to a teacher of rhetoric. In a later letter (see below, 29) she says that she is running both her paternal home and her husband's home. Why this should be the case we cannot unravel from the little information given us in the extant sources. The letter fills less than two printed pages.

Summary. She describes a walk she and her mother took over the family estate. There were beautiful meadows with flowers, running streams, and chattering birds. Along the way, shepherds played on pipe and reed, with sheep and cattle all around. A young girl charmed them with a sweet song of mythical countries. Others played harps. The common people beat their feet to the rhythm. In a grove sacred to Venus, nymphs played with delight. The goodwill of the country filled their souls. Goodwill would fill me more often, Cereta concludes, if you would visit more frequently. ❧

15. To Constantine Boniface

(September 5, 1485 or February 5, 1486) Vt 30, T 23

This is the first of two letters to Constantine Boniface (for the other see below, 25), who is unknown to me from other sources. The letter is one of several instances in which the sources do not agree on date. Tomasini gives the earlier date (which is where the letter is placed in this listing), Vt the later one. The letter fills one printed page.

Summary. She knows that she is supposed to respond to his letter with an eloquence that equals his, but she is unequal to the task. Since love is not based on utility she will forego the attempt entirely and simply send him her love [a diplomatic way of declining to write anything substantive]. ❧

16. *To Dominico Patusio, Lawyer*
(September 10, 1485) Vt 13, T 4, Ve 12

This is the only letter addressed to this lawyer, unknown to me from other sources. It fills over one printed page.

Summary. She acknowledges receipt of a recent invitation to her from him. She values him, she says, because of his relationship to her husband Peter, and on behalf of her family accepts his invitation to attend a celebration at his home. They will all come on the day before the feast of the cross and will plan to have a happy time. She thanks him for his kindness and asks his indulgence for her dull letter. ❧

17. *To Francis Prandonus*
(September 10, 1485) Vt 18, T 9, Ve 17

This is the first of two letters (for the other see below, 18), to this lawyer, unknown to me from other sources. The letter fills less than one printed page.

Summary. Her husband is about to return home. She is supposed to have written Prandonus in his behalf but has until now failed to do so. She hopes that he will respond quickly so that the matter in question [see 18, below] can be resolved by the time her husband returns. ❧

18. *To Francis Prandonus*
(September 12, 1485) Vt 16, T 7, Ve 15

See above, 17. The request referred to in that letter is made clear here. The letter fills one printed page.

Summary. Her husband, Peter Serina, departed for Venice with the money from an endowment and has left behind documents of agreement to repay. She requests that Prandonus represent him and is confident that he will act in their best interests. ❧

19. *To Paul Zane, Bishop of Brescia*
(September 22, 1485) Vt 2, Ve 2

For text, see below, V. This letter was published by a Brescian historian: Agostino Zanelli, "Laura Cereta al Vescovo Zane," *Brixia*

Sacra, XIV, 1923, pp. 173–78. There are no notes. Paul Zane, to whom the letter is addressed, was born in 1460 and elected bishop of Brescia in 1480, succeeding Lorenzo Zane, his uncle (some said his father). He occupied the position from May 24, 1481 until his death in March 1531. He was apparently a worldly cleric, emulating the Renaissance papacy of his time. See *Storia di Brescia: II. La dominazione Veneta (1426–1575)*, promossa e diretta da Giovanni Treccani degli Alfieri (Brescia: Morcelliana, 1963), pp. 418–20. On the dates of his bishopric, see Pius Bonifacius Gams, *Series Episcoporum Ecclesiae Catholicae* (Graz: Akademische Druck, 1957), p. 780. The letter is entitled "On the Neglected Eucharist: A Complaint."

Summary. The Roman Church venerates images even as was done by the Hebrews in the Old Testament. Moses, for example, created the image of a serpent that could aid those bitten by a real serpent. In Rome there are many images, e.g., Veronica's veil on which the image of Christ is imprinted. The same was true among the Romans and Greeks. The Romans placed the image of Jove, among other things, in a temple to be watched over by the Vestal Virgins. Alexander of Macedon kept the sweet-smelling perfume of Darius in an ark. Christians honor the wood of the cross and the thorns of Jesus as the Romans honored their household gods. Churches are filled with the bones of apostles and martyrs. All these things are guarded as the Venetians guard their wealth. But the Eucharist is not guarded. It is open to all. No bolts or guards keep people away, so that the body and blood of Jesus' humanity can be trampled on by anyone. Is this as it should be? What opinion must one hold in this matter? ❧

20. To Peter Stella

(September 23, 1485) Vt 24, T 15, Ve 23

This is the only letter to this correspondent, who is otherwise unknown to me. It fills less than one printed page.

Summary. She refers to a letter she wrote to him not long ago, a letter composed in the middle of the night when she was drowsy and her mind was hallucinating. How could he admire her if she was thus induced to make mistakes? She knows, however, that even though he could take her letter apart bit by bit, the fact that she wrote it will induce him to accept it. ❧

21. *To Regimund Fortunatus, Natural Philosopher*
(Oct. 15, 1485) Vt 69, T 57, Ve 59

This is the only letter to this correspondent, who is unknown to me from other sources. The letter has a title, "The Influences of the Planets on Living Things," and fills about four printed pages. I am grateful to Ms. Joan Tiley, a student of mine, for information regarding the various plants mentioned by Cereta.

Summary. The sun, moon, and fixed stars all play a role in the regulation of nature. Moreover, each plant has its planetary ruler. Saturn governs asphodali [a white or yellow flower like a daffodil which has medicinal uses], Jupiter rules eupatorus [hemp agrimony, used in the Middle Ages as an aid to digestion and against constipation, as well as to remove stray earwigs from the ears], Mars rules plantago [it had a reputation for healing wounds, assuaging tertian and quartan fevers, and curing bites from mad dogs], cichorea is ruled by the Sun [chicory, a tonic, laxative], verbena is ruled by Venus [highly regarded for its scent from ancient times, an antiseptic helpful in disorders of the nervous system], the Moon rules paeonia [peony: Apollo used this flower to cure the wounds of the gods], salvia is ruled by Aries [sage: popular in the Middle Ages, it spread through Europe because Charlemagne advised its cultivation; medicinal value was believed to be contained in its leaves], cyclamen is ruled by Leo, artemisia is ruled by Scorpio [mugwort and wormwood, which overcome inflammatory swellings, kidney stones, gout and rheumatism], aristolochia is ruled by Pisces [a very strong plant which Pliny says could not be used in garlands and laudatory crowns; because of its power to cause organ damage and even death it lost its popularity], but it should be used only cautiously. Thus there is a relation between plants and the constellations of the heavenly bodies, just as there is between the birth of a person and the same heavenly bodies. Plants are most efficaciously used when the constellations are right for each of them. There are other influences on character of which Xenocrates has spoken. However, her interest in the magic of drugs is not intended to turn people away from custom but rather to assure knowledge of these things in the community. ❧

22. *To Albert de Albertis*

(October 15, 1485) Vt 23, T 14, Ve 22

See above, 8. The letter fills less than two printed pages.

Summary. She is afraid her silence has inflamed his anger, for he has written nothing to her and even seems to have withdrawn. Her own failure to write has been the result of necessities imposed on her, and she feels that should generate pity rather than anger in him. Should he accept her again, she would send more and longer letters to him. ❧

23. *To Clement Longulus, Grammarian*

(October 31, 1485) Vt 26, T 17, Ve 25

This is the first of two letters to Longulus (see below, 66), doubtless a teacher of rhetoric, but unknown to me from other sources. The letter is significant because it is one of only two instances in which Cereta displays a knowledge of Greek (see below, 43). It is also the first letter to make reference to the criticism of envious detractors, a theme that increases in importance as these letters continue. The letter fills less than one printed page.

Summary. She has spoken openly, not in veiled language, whatever her detractors might say. She admits that she has always had detractors as well as adulators and believes both are equally injurious to credibility [cf. below, 41]. His opinion of her should not be governed by what others say. ❧

24. *To Albert de Albertis*

(October 31, 1485) Vt 68, T 55, Ve 57

See above, 8. The astrological data provided in this letter make it possible to pinpoint the date as 1485. I am indebted to Ms. Joan Tiley, a student of mine, for making this determination. This letter is entitled "On the Correlation of the Heavenly Bodies with the Birth of Men." Like other letters in her corpus that are titled, it is of some length, in this case about four printed pages.

Summary. He has written her [perhaps in response to 21, above], and praised her lavishly, in contrast to his earlier rejection of her letters. But a gift should never be refused. Her gift is his horoscope for his forty-eighth year.

On that date Saturn will ascend into the eleventh house of Sagittarius. Jupiter will be breaking away from the north into the tenth house of Capricorn. Burning Mars will be declining from the star in back of Aquarius. But the Sun will enter the eleventh house of Aries. Venus will be climbing to Boreas following the tail of Taurus. Mercury will be in the twenty-fourth house of Pisces. The tail of Scorpio will carry the Moon into opposition with Venus. All these positions are very important. For they tell us which planet has dominion in a given house and which oppositions of them occur before birth. The constellation at one's birth is especially important as a presentiment of divine will. However, the influences of the heavens are not decisive, because some things always remain unknown to us. ❧

25. To Constantine Boniface
(November 10, 1485) Vt 74, T 62, Ve 64

See above, 15. The letter fills less than two printed pages.

Summary. We have here a rather formal thank you letter for gifts received. In this case the gifts are food: pears, grape wine, fish, eggs, chestnuts, mushrooms, figs, olives. These gifts concord with Boniface's bountifulness, to which first place is conceded. ❧

26. To Michael Baetus
(December 12, 1485) Vt 28, T 21

Michael Baetus is addressed variously by Cereta in her correspondence as Michaeli, Michaeli Ba, Michaeli Baeto, Michaeli Carrariensi, and Michaeli Clarensi. He is addressed consistently as *physicus*, "natural philosopher." He is unknown to me from other sources. For other letters to him, see below, 42, 43, and 47. This letter fills over one printed page.

Summary. She acknowledges receipt of several letters some time ago [none extant]. Although previously she has repaid him in kind, she has not until now answered these particular letters. She desires to do so, however, for one does not readily come upon trustworthy philosophers. In the future, their correspondence should be based on reciprocal gifts. ❧

27. *To Helena Caesarea*
(December 20, 1485) Vt 8, Ve 7

For text, see below, VI. Helena Caesarea is unknown to me from other sources. The letter is entitled "On the Coming of the Turks."

Summary. Cereta seems alarmed that the Turks have crossed over into Apulia in southern Italy [this actually happened in 1480, though she writes as if the event is virtually contemporary with this letter]. Does it not seem that the fall of Constantinople can be heard even now? When they conquer, there is no reverence for noble women, holy virgins, or religion. Should they descend upon us, we can expect no better treatment. If past experience is projected into the future, our condition would be one of hopelessness in which death would be our only respite. However, she is not like Cassandra, the daughter of Priam, who would prophesy the fall of her country. She looks only at what has happened, not at what might happen. Her strategy: We should renounce the pomp of the age and place our trust in the Lord, who has saved the faithful in the past from catastrophes of every kind. ❧

28. *To Felix Tadinus, Natural Philosopher*
(December 31, 1485) Vt 4, Ve 3

For text, see below, VII. Cereta wrote three letters to this correspondent (see below, 47 and 57) who is unknown to me from other sources. She consistently addresses him as "natural philosopher." Both of the other letters to him refer to her husband's death, and one of them is among the first she wrote following that event. As the body of this letter suggests, she had known him for some time (perhaps his son also was taught by her father). Her letters to him span all the three years during which her "published" letters were composed.

Summary. Deucalion and Pyrrha were saved, following the universal flood, by floating in an ark, and they filled the earth again with men and women by throwing rocks over their shoulders. She is looking for such a rebirth of friendship out of the silence which Felix has imposed on himself. Her father has always been gracious to him, and yet he apparently rejects the entire family, inasmuch as he has not responded to their letters. She implores him to return, if only as Eurydice, brought back to the gates of hell by Orpheus' gentle songs. ❧

29. To Sigismund de Buccis, Doctor of Laws
(January 1, 1486) Vt 11, T 2, Ve 10

This is Cereta's only letter to this correspondent, who is unknown to me from other sources. The letter fills over four printed pages.

Summary. Her marriage leaves her torn between duties to her paternal family and the concerns of marriage. Despite her many duties, she continues to find time for study, largely by sleeping very little. She works from late at night until early morning. This letter itself was long in the writing, and it would seem that the labor spent in producing it is not justified by the outcome. And yet women spend even more time embroidering rich designs on their dresses, and then displaying themselves in their rich attire, wasting their time and their talents [see below, 54]. Her labor has produced a large volume of letters. Giving up the pursuit of transitory riches with which others are concerned, she is consumed with love for literature and the fame it may bring, and is driven on in this quest by the zeal of her father. ❧

30. To Silvester, her Father
(February 1, 1486) Vt 27, T 18, Ve 26

Cereta's father was her teacher, perhaps her only real mentor in classical studies. She pays constant tribute to him, though this is her only letter to him. One of the charges against her was that her father wrote her letters (see below, 63). Despite his central role in her life, not only as her teacher, but, as reflected in this letter, the most important male supporter of her efforts to achieve stature as a humanist writer, we know nothing about his education. It must certainly have included the subjects which he taught her so thoroughly—philosophy, mathematics, sacred literature, and classical Greek and Latin. His mathematical knowledge we can infer from his central role in fortifying towns allied to Brescia in the conflicts of the early 1480s, mentioned by Cereta in 35 below. He probably died late in 1488, for during that year he is listed in the *Provisioni* of the city of Brescia as a citizen qualified for public office, but as deceased. He may have died shortly after that list was promulgated, or shortly before. In any case, he is not mentioned in the next publication of that list in December 1490. His death provides a *terminus ad quem* for Cereta's correspondence, for given his importance in her life, his death would not have passed unmentioned or unlamented had he died while she was writing these letters. As I suggest in Part One, his death may have been an important reason for her discontinuing her efforts as a humanist. The letter fills two printed pages.

Summary. She has left the circle at the convent of Chiara, because envy had so caught hold of her peers that they were making her sick with their criticism. They challenged her to an exchange of letters, thinking they could easily overcome her. But they wrote hastily and did not succeed. They make excuses for their shortcomings and conceal their lack of learning by attacking her. She wants her father to be the judge. If he compares her letter to theirs he will see that her work is superior. ❧

31. To Albert de Albertis

(February 3, 1486) Vt 28, T 22

See above, 8. Cereta is not in Brescia but somewhere in the country when she writes this letter, as must also have been the case for 30 above. The letter fills two printed pages.

Summary. In her leisure she wanders about the farms. She apologizes for not having written him for a long time [since 24 above, on October 31, 1485?]. She is breaking her silence now, even though it has been very difficult to do so. She has started and stopped more than once. She hopes he will overlook the rusticity of her pen, seeing that she lives in the midst of uncultivated people, common discourse, and horse dung. ❧

32. To Peter Zenus Patavius

(February 3, 1486) Vt 76, T 64, Ve 66

First paragraph unedited; reproduced in a note in the Table of Letters, above, where this letter is listed. This is the only letter to this correspondent, who is unknown to me from other sources. The letter is entitled "Opinion about entering into the bond of marriage," and is more akin to a formal oration than to a letter, filling eight printed pages.

There are discernible sections to this letter/oration. The first is an introduction discussing marriage in relation to the heavenly constellations. The second, and by far the longest section, is devoted to examples of faithfulness in marriage, as well as of women in general (whether daughters or mothers or wives), mostly taken from classical literature. The final section discusses the relations of husband and wife as these make a marriage prosper or falter.

Summary. When Venus and Pisces are joined in the heavens, the time is favorable for marriage. In some cultures auspices are also important for obtaining a favorable marriage, e.g., the sacrifice of a turtledove. But if one takes no account either of the stars' positions or of auspices, then perhaps examples of the purity of women in the past will be persuasive.

Dido chose death rather than widowhood. Penelope waited for twenty years for Ulysses' return. Sulpicia chose to go into exile in Sicily with her husband Lentulus. Hippo Graece, a nymph, and youngest daugher of Ocean and Tethys, preserved her chastity by drowning rather than allowing violation by sailors.

There is the example of Antigone, who buried her brother Polynices against the order of her uncle Creon, King of Argos. Of mothers, Veturia softened the anger of Coriolanus which no one else had been able to do. Nero made his mother co-regent with him because she poisoned Claudius with a mushroom.

There are examples also of courageous widows. Marpissa and Lampedo, warlike widows, chose death by the sword rather than live under foreign conquerors. Portia, imitating the constancy of her father Cato, killed herself after the death of her beloved Decius Brutus. Julia, born to Julius Caesar, so loved Pompey that when he died she suddenly collapsed and followed him into death. And after the death of Drusus, Antonia spent her life in lamentation. After C. Marius had murdered their husbands, the Cimbrian wives hung themselves on the same night. Among the Hebrews, Judith cut off the head of Holofernes.

These examples [and others which have not been included] should encourage one to marriage, for they demonstrate with what constancy men and women are often united. In addition, nature inclines toward the propagation of its own kind and reproduces our characteristics in our offspring. Further, the church makes of marriage a sacrament. For all these reasons, marriage is well approved.

Marriage imposes obedience upon people, and this softens the force of domestic schisms. It consoles us in the face of death and overcomes anger with mercy and joy. Husbands, however, should treat their wives with gentleness. Some violate the marriagebed because their marriagebed is unhappy, some submit but in a way that is destructive. ❧

33. To Bernard di Leno, Cousin

(February 26, 1486) Vt 41, T 34, Ve 36

This is the only letter to her cousin, who is unknown to me from other sources. The second half of the letter contains some important autobiographical statements. The letter fills two printed pages.

Summary. In a previous letter to her uncle, Ludovico di Leno [see above, 2], she described the stars on the family shield. Now she proposes to clarify the origins of the family name. The shield shows a marble statue engraved with the letters Lenus. On either side are two erect lions supporting the entrance to a temple. A third lion sits on top of the entrance. He is even more savage than lions generally are. Thus it is as if our noble family were descended from kings, having on its shield the king of beasts.

Turning abruptly from this description, she says that she turned away from things which generally preoccupy women and to a love of literature. This was the only means of achieving the fame she desires, and although she has not reached the pinnacle, her growth has been sufficient to satisfy her thus far. She has spent seven years in this pursuit of learning. [At the moment of writing she is almost seventeen, so that by this account she would have begun at the age of nine. This is corroborated by her autobiographical account in letter 50, below.] Once she had advanced sufficiently in her studies she began to write these letters. She recognizes that her knowledge is not great, but she has written of what she knows, and in a way that is not tasteless. ❧

34. To Holy Pelegrina

(February 26, 1486) Vt 54, T 47a, Ve 49

This is the only letter to this correspondent, who is unknown to me from other sources. She is clearly a learned woman who, in that capacity, had come into conflict with Cereta. The conflict appears similar to that with Cereta's male detractors (see below, 60). The letter fills about two printed pages.

Summary. Those who write about friendship are all agreed that it is excellent and continuous. This is no wonder, since that which is excellent should always be maintained. But our friendship failed, Cereta says, even though nurtured by mutual love. Why? Because you have gossiped about my lack of learning. What you should rather do is undertake literary work similar to mine. If we keep truth in sight we will remember that between friends there is never a victory of one over the other. We must come to terms with the question between us so that the holy covenant of our mutual respect, now broken, may be restored. Cereta is ready to forget the offense and heal the rift through forgiveness. The common attachment both have to literature should strengthen the ties between them.

35. To Ludovico Cendrata of Verona
(March 15, 1486) Vt 81, T 69, Ve 71

Ludovico Cendrata of Verona was a relative and student of Guarino da Verona, and a friend of Francesco Barbaro, Isotta Nogarola (with whom he corresponded) and other humanists. He edited the histories of Josephus (1480). According to Cosenza, 236 of his letters are extant in various manuscripts (see Mario Emilio Cosenza, *Biographical and Bibliographical Dictionary of the Italian Humanists and of the World of Classical Scholarship in Italy, 1300–1800* [2nd ed.], 6 vols. [Boston: G. K. Hall, 1962], Vol. II, 961; Vol. I, item 476). I have not been able to search these to determine whether or not he wrote to Cereta, though the *Iter Italicum* yielded nothing in this respect.

This is the only letter to Cendrata in the Cereta corpus. It bears the title "Complaint about the Beginning and Causes of War, about the Brescian War and about Celestial Portents." It fills seven printed pages.

Summary. The god Mars virtually controls the world, as have the war gods of other peoples before the Greeks and Romans. And poets have long sung of the deeds of war gods and warriors, as Homer sang of the overthrow of the Trojans. Books are yet to be written about the cruel deeds of Cyrus, the Arabs, the Gauls, and the Goths. These conflicts come from the desire for domination, and since this is perennial, concern with war never ceases. The hope of conquest has drawn thousands of unknown warriors to their deaths.

In the areas surrounding Brescia also a conflict recently ensued. An army attacked our borders and plundered some villages. Populations retreated into the larger cities, leaving the countryside deserted. Fortifications were built or strengthened. Some panicked and surrendered to the enemy. But most remained constant. The winter came, stopping the fighting, but with its passing the war resumed once more. Farms were seized and burned. A monstrous fear of the enemy began to permeate the country. Again some surrendered or joined the enemy, but most were courageous and the cities survived.

All this was five years ago. Cereta remembers it, because she drove to various cities with her father who was in charge of widening ditches and fortifying walls and watch towers. He also watched the signs of the zodiac for their portents. One portent he saw was a fire burning as if poured forth from Mars or some star [a comet?]. Cereta asks Ludovico how he would interpret this (if indeed he places any trust in astrology). ❧

36. To Jacob Basiliscus

(April 29, 1486) Vt 56, T 47b, Ve 51

This is the only letter to this correspondent, who is unknown to me from other sources. It fills less than one printed page.

Summary. She acknowledges receipt of his eloquent letters and orations. What else is encountered in them except Cicero? What shines in the narration unless a rhetorician? What glitters in the epilogue except the best judgments devised by reason? The divisions are all there, the material is adorned with illustations. Finally, the oration returned from whence it began, so that all things in it are synthesized. [This is indication of the practice she follows in her own oration. A number of her letters subsequent to this one, just as a few prior to it, are more or less formal orations.] ❧

37. To Albert de Albertis

(May 7, 1486) Vt 39, T 32, Ve 34

See above, 8. The letter is written on the occasion of his retirement from public office, perhaps that of judge. It fills one-half a printed page.

Summary. Albert has lived with integrity and all in the city have benefited from his integrity. As he leaves office, he does so with the praise of all rather than with money. He has, in sum, preferred justice to utility, which in turn prepares him for an eternal reward. His future should therefore be a happy one. ❧

38. To John Olivieri or Angelo Capello
(June 5, 1486) Vt 21, T 12, Ve 20

In Tomasini this letter is addressed to Angelo Capello, but in Vt and Ve to John Olivieri, the grammarian (see above, 7). This was one of two letters published by Ottavio Rossi, *Elogi istorici di Bresciani illustri*, 1620, pp. 225-29. Rossi copies from his own manuscript which was the one used by Tomasini. Hence the addressee is Angelo Capriolo or Capello. In his biographical note, Rossi says that he was a Carmelite doctor of theology and also learned in mathematics. This is the only letter in Tomasini addressed to him (there are none in the other two sources). The letter deals largely with the constellations of the heavens and so it would seem reasonable that it might have been addressed to Capello or Capriolo, given his interest in mathematics. On the other hand, there are other letters (see below, 39) addressed to Olivieri which deal with the same theme. Moreover, the reference to the recipient's farmland points to Olivieri, since a Carmelite monk would not have owned land. The astrological information provided in the letter is specific enough to enable a precise determination of the year date as 1486. I am indebted to a student of mine, Ms. Joan Tiley, for making this determination. The letter fills four printed pages.

Summary. He may be astonished that a young girl, instructed in a few works of literature, should have dared to write to such an eminent man. But his virtue persuaded her. Like him, she is not satisfied with opinion, but must know the teachings of the heavenly bodies in order to discern the will of God and allay her inner anxieties. She writes this in the country away from urban buildings and in proximity to his fields.

On this day Saturn, that old man of the planets, is retrograde to the west, descending to Boreas. Jupiter is declining to the north. While Saturn is cold and dry, Jupiter is warm and humid. But Jupiter is proceeding to frigid Capricorn where it will cause rain. Mars, dry and fiery, receding from its hot conjunction with the Sun and accelerating south, approaches the third house of Aries. The Sun is in the fourth house, burned up in its dryness, and will move to the eleventh house of Cancer. Venus is following the Sun wandering retrograde to the west and sees the Great and Little Bear constellations. Mercury follows the orbit of the Sun in the fifth house and attracts the dryness of burning Leo. The Moon, watery in its coldness and humidity, will be controlled by the dryness of burning Aries in the fourth position of the first house. The conjunction of the Moon with Jupiter and of Mercury with Saturn, will cause farms to be cultivated. ❧

39. To John Olivieri
(June 7, 1486) Vt 10, T 1, Ve 9

See above, 7. This is the only letter written by Cereta herself which bears a year date as well as a month and day date. The letter fills less than two printed pages.

Of the brothers mentioned in this letter, Basil and Daniel, the latter was, like his sister, well-known in local literary circles. He became a physician and wrote a poem *De foro et laudibus Brixiae* in which he praised all the famous citizens of Brescia during his day, including his father and sister. The poem was written a few years after Laura's death. Gianmaria Mazzuchelli, who published this poem in 1778, asserts that Daniel Cereta died in 1528.

Summary. Saturn is behind in the sixth house. Jupiter is retrograde in the eighth house of Capricorn. Mars is in the twenty-first house, with Aries. Venus, now close to the earth, is very bright and dependent upon Gemini in the nineteenth house. And so on. The point is that the positions of the heavenly bodies favor the study of arts and letters. Since the stars are favorable, he should receive her brothers, Basil and Daniel, as students in his celebrated school. ❧

40. To John Olivieri
(June 13, 1486) Vt 25, T 16, Ve 24

See above, 7. The letter fills over two printed pages.

Summary. This is a letter of thanks for a dinner Cereta attended at the Olivieri home. She describes the setting as like feasts in Rome and the company as like the Muses or Plato's *Symposium* where constant discourse was the order of the day. The academy was covered with tapestries on all sides, and the banquet table filled with renowned wines, figs, fowl, fruit, meats on ice, sheep smoked on a spit. Cereta especially commends his wife for having shown such skill. He should, however, she concludes, temper his liberality with frugality lest he encourage gluttony. ❧

41. To Diana Cereta, her sister
(July 1, 1486) Vt 22, T 13, Ve 21

This is the only letter Cereta wrote to her younger sister. (She also had another sister, Deodata, to whom she wrote in letter 76 below, as well as the three brothers we have encountered above, letters 7, 9, and 39.) Cereta herself at the time of writing was just under seventeen and her sister could not have been more than twelve or thirteen. Yet her sister must have entered the same path of learning Cereta herself did, as suggested by the content of the letter. The letter fills two printed pages.

Summary. Cereta refers to several recent letters from her sister in which Diana praised her excessively for her learning, calling her a sister of Apollo, among other things. The truth would be better than such fictions. Cereta knows she is not worthy of such praise. In public Diana should be more cautious lest she perjure herself. Cereta does not wish to be pushed too quickly to high honor, for those rise higher who rise more slowly. Industry requires time to bear fruit. Furthermore, virtue rather than the pleasure of study should be regarded as of greatest importance. It is enough to have entered the path of knowledge. ❧

42. To Michael Baetus
(July 6, 1486) Vt 7, Ve 6

For text, see below, VIII. See above, 26, and below, 43.

Summary. Cereta is upset at having been accused of borrowing what she wrote to Baetus from some book. She admits that what she knows she has learned from others, but she protests that she too is an astrologer. Moreover, she has learned what she has, not in order to parade it before the world, but in order to be a model of virtue. To allay his suspicion of plagiarism, she proposes to describe the heavens for the four days immediately preceding this letter.

The Moon has passed from Leo to Virgo, is 90 degrees from Saturn and retrograde from Jupiter, and about 120 degrees from Mars. In this position Jupiter generates friendship. But hatred flows from Mars and even more from Saturn. It is a time of purgation. Virgo is in the south. The Moon, shadowy in nature, is 9 degrees ahead of the Sun, in the house of Venus and not far from the rising of Mercury. In retrograde Saturn there is a harmonious connection between cold and dry, where the fixed star Algaphar appears in the Arctic. ❧

43. To Michael Baetus

(July 8, 1486) Vt 43, T 36, Ve 38

See above, 26 and 42. The letter fills one printed page.

Summary. Her mathematical knowledge is limited. She does not know arithmetic or geometry to the extent of being able to decide the magnitude of the celestial orbits and the spaces between them. Pythagoras wrote that the body of the Sun is eight times that of the earth. About such things she cannot pronounce. Nonetheless, her pen is not rustic, for she has studied rather than given herself to leisure. ❧

44. To Peter Serina, Consort

(July 17, 1486) Vt 15, T 6, Ve 14

See above, 3. This is the last letter Cereta wrote to her husband, and it is particularly poignant, for he died shortly after this letter was written, of the plague, for which cause he is mourning the death of his brother discussed in this letter. The letter fills one printed page.

Summary. Peter's brother, Nicholas, has died of the plague and Peter is distraught. But Cereta reminds him that nature destines all to die and that death is not an evil for a good person. But even if Nicholas lived an evil life, Peter should not have behaved at the funeral by tearing his hair, shouting, or beating his breast. His wailing will not restore Nicholas to life. Moreover, she and Peter are bound by a higher allegiance than death. Husband and wife should love each other for a lifetime. She exhorts him to turn from his grief, for he is dearer to her than Nicholas. ❧

45. To John Olivieri

(August 1, 1486) Vt 40, T 33, Ve 35

See above, 7. The letter fills less than one printed page.

Summary. Gallus, an orator as well as an astrologer, fell into a ditch while gazing at the stars. Why did she, a girl not so learned, fall into a ditch when she also was trying to measure the stars? She is willing to confess her errors; if they are infrequent that is due to the grace of God. ❧

46. To Albert de Albertis
(August 5, 1486) Vt 34, T 27, Ve 29

See above, 8. The Cereta corpus is exactly divided between letters composed before and those composed after the death of her husband. This was the first she wrote after her "recent loss" and reflects an immediacy of grief, as do the two following it. The letter fills two printed pages.

Summary. She thanks Albert for his long friendship to her family, but his exhortations have nonetheless had little effect in relieving her tortured mind. Her grief has so overcome her that she no longer knows whether she prefers to live or die. She reflects that those children are happy who die in infancy. She would prefer to be like the Atlantides [descendants of Atlas] who believed that their brother Hyas had been carried away to a star, or like Alcyon who believed that Ceyx had been changed into a bird, or like Hecuba, the wife of Priam, who was changed into a dog after the king and the kingdom had been lost. Yes, she longs for death, even the death of a pagan, since it appears impossible for her to live with the freedom of a Christian. Perhaps the gods will grant her request to die. ❧

47. To Felix Tadinus
(August 10, 1486) Vt 32, T 25, Ve 27

See above, 28. This letter carries the title "The Image of Death" and follows the preceding letter in depth of feeling and immediacy of anguish. It fills more than one printed page.

Summary. Felix's letter consoled her, but nonetheless the grief that rages in her heart is so great that whenever she thinks about it she begins to weep again, as if the spirit of death were flying about inside her. She longs for death, indeed, at this moment nothing would please her more. For what enjoyment can follow the victory of death? None. All that remains is to increase the misery of dying even more. ❧

48. To Michael Baetus
(August 13, 1486) Vt 34, T 26, Ve 28

See above, 26. The letter fills one printed page.

Summary. Both kindness and copiousness show forth in his recent letters, but he must remember that the eloquence of her pen has been silenced by death. A perverse fate has struck down her husband and brought her to the point of longing for death. Only death can erase her recent misery. Already her health has been impaired by her grief. ❧

49. To Brother Thomas of Milan

(September 10, 1486 or October 21, 1486) Vt 60, T 52, Ve 54

The correspondence with Brother Thomas is among the most important in the Cereta corpus. Three letters to him are preserved in all the sources (in addition to this letter, see below, 73 and 78) and in addition, Vt preserves three letters from him to Cereta (below, 72, 74 and 75) and one to Cereta's father Silvester (below, 68). These four letters by Brother Thomas (edited below, Part Three) are the only letters preserved in the Cereta corpus not written by Cereta herself.

Brother Thomas is unknown to me from other sources than these letters. He seems to have been educated in both the scholastic and humanist traditions. He was not Cereta's teacher but in some sense her spiritual adviser. These and other details of his life, together with an analysis of his relationship to Cereta, are presented in Part One, above.

This letter, like those immediately preceding, presupposes the death of her husband. But her attitude is changing. She no longer longs for death but for God; she has given up the quest for fame and is turning more towards religion. Quite clearly, in this longer letter (over four printed pages) she is overcoming her grief through her literary labors.

Summary. She has gotten great delight from reading the works of Augustine and Jerome, though she is not far enough advanced to be considered their disciple. Indeed, she is unable to articulate on paper what she has gotten from them, but she can see already that judged by their work, her own is empty. She regards Brother Thomas as unjust, however, when he charges that there is too little Christianity in her writings and that they are dangerous. She aspires to be neither an orator nor a theologian. How could she penetrate mysteries which Thomas, Dionysius, and many other learned men wore themselves out trying to understand? She does not wish to struggle against God by contemplating something laborious but rather to believe [see below, 75]. Nor does she think she can understand the mysteries contained in the immense heavenly bodies. But there is one law, one word of God, and one virtue which ought to be diffused in our hearts, namely, that God inspires us with his love. God, not death, is what she now longs for.

The thought of judgment and resurrection should be paramount. For this reason, she says, she has renounced the quest for the brief and fallen glory of this world which generates pride of wisdom and separates us from true religion. She will seek self-knowledge in humility and so prepare herself for eternal life.

All these thoughts have been generated by Brother Thomas's exhortations to her and by the death of her husband, which has rendered her so sad and anxious. She sometimes longs for the monastic security she once knew [see below, 50]. She will await the form of God's mercy and compassion with patience. ❧

50. To Nazaria Olympia

(November 5, 1486) Vt 71, T 59, Ve 61

This is the only letter to this correspondent, who is unknown to me from other sources. It is an autobiographical letter, carrying the title "Digest of her own Life" and written at the request of the correspondent. It is important for many of the details we have about Cereta's education. It fills about eight printed pages.

Summary. She is complying with Nazaria's request for details about her life because of their friendship and her respect for Nazaria's great virtue. She does not, however, have much leisure for such things. Perhaps, she reflects, she wrote better when she did not have so many cares pressing upon her. She does not study now with the same ardor she once had. She is more withdrawn and morose, and her style reflects this. What follows will therefore be a simple narrative in which posterity will be little interested [i.e., presumably, since her style is no longer ornate, her writing will not lead to her immortality, as she had earlier hoped].

She was born during the fourth month which precedes the year 1470 [i.e., August or September 1469] and named after a laurel tree which stood outside her parents' home. She was the firstborn child and, perhaps for this reason, well loved by all.

Her nurse, Montana, caressed her like a mother, but Montana's monstrous face (her throat was swollen with gout) frightened her. To this day Cereta sees her face as if it were a ghost.

She learned very little during the first seven years of her life. Then she was sent to live with nuns for two years. Her principal occupation in the convent was embroidering with a needle – she learned to weave very complicated patterns. During her second year she imbibed a religious spirit. She was also taught, however, the rudiments of reading and writing. After two years she returned home to everyone's great joy.

At this point her father became her teacher. Especially from the age of eleven she applied herself, studying grammar and rhetoric. At the age of twelve many domestic duties devolved upon her, but this did not diminish the time devoted to study. She turned to mathematics and from thence to religious subjects. In all this, she was filled with the greatest happiness.

Having scarcely passed the age of fifteen she was married to a merchant who died after they had been married only eighteen months, an event which threw her into utter confusion. She knew that he, like all of us, must die. But his death was so untimely that it will always be a source of sadness and misery for her.

She was once delighted by the study of the heavens. Now, however, she prefers to ignore the fate which is in store for her rather than to know it. In any case, the same God is ruler over all things, and his will is to be done. Desire for knowledge of his will is more rash than is good for humans. She therefore beseeches Nazaria not to long to know things that are to come, but rather to leave those things to God and to place her hope in the gospel, so that Christ, the true Son of God, may open for her the marriage of paradise. ❧

51. To Barbara Alberta

(November 21 or 26, 1486) Vt 72, T 60, Ve 62

This is the only letter to this correspondent, who is unknown to me from other sources. The letter is entitled "On the Instability of Fortune and Congratulations on her Marriage." It fills three to four printed pages. The Vatican MS dates this letter November 21 while Ve and T date it November 26.

Summary. She congratulates Barbara on her forthcoming marriage, commends her virtue, and singles out her tranquillity of mind as a strength she should never allow fate to take from her. She herself was robbed of her tranquillity by the death of her husband, whose memory still brings tears to her eyes. They were, she says, joined in a love for literature and in peace before death took him from her, leaving her miserable. People do many things to assuage their grief: travel, seek wealth, fight wars. But in Cereta's heart only love of literature rages. Her mind finds its pleasure in study which is conducive to virtue inasmuch as it avoids luxury and leads to God. She exhorts Barbara to die to this world [as she has?] so that she may better endure it, though she admits that she is saying this more for her own sake than for Barbara's. She concludes with the comment that marriage has been happy for her parents, and she hopes it will also be so for Barbara. ❧

52. To Julianus Trosculus
(November 30, 1486) Vt 50, T 43, Ve 45

This is the only letter to this correspondent, who is unknown to me from other sources. The letter is entitled "Consolation on the Death of his little Daughter," and fills three to four printed pages.

Summary. Cereta describes the scene at Julianus's home three days after the birth of his daughter. Everyone was well and happy. The child was rosy and beautifully formed. After a long visit everyone left, and shortly afterwards the child died of a sudden sickness, turning the happiness of all into misery. Cereta confesses that she has never suffered the loss of a child, because she has never given birth, but she has suffered the loss of a loved one and knows that, however many his tears, they will not alleviate the sorrow of death. None of us can have a certain assurance that she will last through the next hour. If one recognizes this, weeping can be kept within bounds. For her part, she would not choose to die because she had lost a daughter. Only those are happy who have come to terms with, and accepted, death as a part of life. ❧

53. To Augustine Aemilius
(February 6, 1487) Vt 37, T 30, Ve 32

This is the first of two letters to this correspondent (see below, 54). Ottavio Rossi (see above, 37), who published 54 below, says nothing about the correspondent, and he is unknown to me from other sources. The letter bears the title "Lamentation" and fills three printed pages.

Summary. There was a time, Cereta says, when she sought to discern causes through astrology. But since the death of her husband the pleasure she once derived from this study has evaporated. Tears have taken the place of study. She asks those who have attacked her to refrain from injuring her further, for death is the sure end of us all.

If Augustine expected eloquence in her he must be disappointed. For although she still thirsts for knowledge her style lacks vitality. ❧

54. To Augustine Aemilius
(February 12, 1487) Vt 38, T 31, Ve 33

See above, 53. This letter bears the title, "Curse against the lifestyle of Women" and is the letter published by Ottavio Rossi in 1620 from his own manuscript later used by Tomasini (see above, 39). The letter fills five printed pages. The theme addressed at length here is alluded to above in 29.

Summary. Cereta describes arriving at the side of her feverish husband as he was dying. In one abominable year she was a girl, bride, and widow, deprived of all the goods of fortune. It is kind of Augustine to consider her his equal, but she does not feel it. Moreover, she is now more zealous for virtue and humility than for honor. Many women contrive arts of adornment and in this way attract men. Antony, for example, was attracted by the adornment of Cleopatra. But Cereta prefers to imitate the integrity of Rebecca. Paris was attracted by Helen; Cereta prefers the modesty of Rachel. Many wives, caught up in displaying themselves, destroy their marriages. In no age has a greater excess of vanity existed than in our own. Women walk through the streets admiring those whose hair is pulled up in knots or whose curls hang down in front or those whose necks are bare or perhaps replete with gold necklaces. The latter, like captives, boast that they are kept by free men. Many display jewels on their fingers. One (her ambition is clear) wears a loose girdle, another pulls her girdle tight. Some wear silken tunics, others sweet-smelling perfumes. The more elegant wear leather shoes and cover their legs as well. They stretch their skin, put softened bread on their faces, paint themselves, and in other ways strive to seem more beautiful by their artificial care than God made them. Is it for this, Cereta asks, that women were begotten? Women should seek honor rather than allurements. They should remember that they are mortal and that those who live and die virtuously will live eternally with God.

Therefore, Augustine should take no cognizance of age or sex. Nature has produced the female sex not from the earth or from a rock, but from the humanity of Adam. Men, who have greater strength than women and therefore more responsibility, should be careful not to misuse their authority and encourage women in the wrong paths. ❧

55. To Cassandra Fedele of Venice

(April 13, 1487) Vt 42, T 35, Ve 37

Cassandra Fedele (1465–1558) wrote letters of her own (though none, so far as I know, to Laura Cereta) and was praised by many of the humanists of her day who corresponded with her. Her letters, like those of Cereta, were edited and published by Tomasini (1636). On her see Margaret L. King, "Thwarted Ambitions: Six Learned Women of the Italian Renaissance," *Soundings* 59 (1976): 295–300 and sources cited, 304. This is the only letter in the Cereta corpus to Cassandra, though she is mentioned as one to whom criticisms of Cereta were addressed by her detractors (see below, 63).

This letter was written in part to display Cereta's knowledge of classical sources. It is the description of a dream in which Cereta descends to the lower world, where she seeks her departed husband. As the conclusion of the letter makes clear, she intends this as a gift of goodwill to Cassandra and hopes that Cassandra will neither scorn it nor flee the labor of responding. The letter fills over five printed pages. For a later judgment on the letter, see below, 67.

Summary. In the center of the lower world fire pours forth and dogs bark at souls approaching the doorstep of Cerberus for the first time. Cereta approaches this door in a dream and is attacked by Charon and driven into the jaws of Orcus. Horror fills her soul as Charon, emitting vile vapors, brings her to the Stygian marsh. She hears sighs all around. Shades of bodies appear. Furies belch forth flames in the form of various kinds of monsters. The Eumenides appear with snakes in their hair. Medusa approaches, excited by these hydrian furies. On one side is swift Acheron and on the other Phlegethon hot with flames. Avernus sends forth a sulphurous odor. Here Tantalus, tortured by hunger and thirst, pants as food and drink continually recede from him. Blind Medusa follows Perseus with dreadful laments. Lethe falls headlong into Tartarus, creating a foamy froth. Pluto roars against Sisyphus. She sees kings presided over by Rhadamanthus. She witnesses wheels of torture, people submerged in boiling pitch, lacerated limbs, and other sights too numerous to describe. There are those who survived the battle of Troy, as well as Jason and Medea. There is Palinurus, Aeneas's pilot, asking for the burial of his discarded body. Priam, who dishonored the altar of Zeus, lies on the right with his hands bound and with blood pouring from his broken neck. Orpheus bewails Eurydice with his lyre. Seeing Tiresias singing oracles she approaches and asks earnestly and sorrowfully about her husband; she is told that he is not there and that she must look to other kingdoms. Whether all this points to something real or not Cereta will not say. She knows only that she was aroused to look forward to seeing her husband elsewhere, perhaps on the Islands of the Blessed.

She writes as she has to Cassandra, not because she is more concerned about a dream than about Cassandra, but rather in order to test the subtlety of Cassandra's intellect with subtle material. She hopes Cassandra will not be covetous but will respond to her. [Given the way Cereta closes this letter, she apparently feared that Cassandra would ignore her—which, presumably, she did.] ❧

56. To Francesca Fontana
(April 13, 1487) Vt 31, T 24

This is the only letter to this correspondent, who is unknown to me from other sources. The letter is entitled "Oration: Curse against Fate." It fills eight printed pages.

Roughly speaking, the oration begins with an introduction which denies Fate, then proceeds to a number of examples (almost half the entire oration) of chance in military affairs, in a briefer section decries in a tomb? Augustus and Julius, the dictators, had no more cause to place their beloved horses in a tomb. Did not the Romans order the crow to be honored with funeral rites because of its capacity to imitate the expression of the human voice?

Soldus then describes his ass, dearer to him than his own life. He bought the creature, of exquisite beauty, with a gold coin, and was almost immediately offered double the price in silver by someone else. Many times he rode on the animal's back. But who will carry him now in his old age? Must he walk on foot? He concludes with a lament on the miseries of old age.

Cereta responds that all grieve for the fate of Soldus. But Soldus' grief is excessive; nothing should cause a temperate man to lose his tranquillity of mind. The memory of the past should not torture him.

Soldus speaks again and describes the violent death of Asellus. While walking on a mountain, the ass slipped and fell down a steep ridge into a valley below where he was attacked by a wolf. How will Soldus and his family find protection now that Asellus is dead? Who will carry home the wood in the cold? Who will carry the crop of wheat?

Once again Cereta speaks, asserting that all share the fate of Asellus and that a sense of desperation is not the response called for. Otherwise, one will be destroyed by grief over, say, the loss of his children. Silence would be better.

Philonacus, a shepherd, makes his way through the throng of people to speak. He had been the keeper of Asellus and has many tales to tell of this ass's life. He describes how the animal learned to pull wagons and carriages so that he could pass through noisy crowds or bad weather without flinching. Unlike others of his species, he was not lazy, but could run with haste without having to be beaten. The stupid animal had a great knowledge of rainstorms, so that the position of his ears was a prophecy of their coming. He serenaded babies at their midday naps. He carried several people on his back when returning from the fields and never threw anyone off, though some fell now and then because of bad horsemanship. Once when he was punished with a beating for refusing to go into a river to wash off, he would not eat or rise for three days. On another occasion, when some boys tried to mount him, he kicked them. As punishment Philonacus tied him to a tree, exposing him to wild beasts. He became so cold and weak that it was only with difficulty that the next day he could be driven home with a cane. These and other incidents make Philonacus feel guilty about his treatment of Asellus. He weeps much more bitterly than Soldus, for he wants absolution. He asks Cereta to illuminate the suffering all this generates with the eloquence of a Demosthenes.

Cereta, in her peroration, also her longest single speech in the dialogue, says that she has spoken as eloquently as she could, though this may not always have proved efficacious, even as Cicero did not always win his cases. If what she has said has not thus far proved effective, all should remember that the soul is immortal. The deeds of Asellus will be remembered long after his death. Finally, both our happiness and our death come from the gods, a thought which should quiet us. Therefore, let reason be restored as ruler over our lives. Lay aside grief and take up the lyre. ❧

2. To Ludovico di Leno

(July 6, 1485) Vt 14, T 5, Ve 13

This is the only letter addressed to her maternal uncle, who is otherwise unknown to me. The di Leno family was long native to Brescia and numbered many among its noble citizens. The letter fills less than two printed pages.

Summary. The shield of the di Leno family contains a constellation of the heavens, the initial inspiration for Cereta's desire to learn astrology. Her study, however, has had as its purpose, not a reward from some Maecenas, but, following the wonderful example of Petrarch, her own eternal fame. For two other reasons also she studies: so that her mind might be possessed of the virtue of excellence and so that she might measure the distances to the stars. ❧

3. To Peter Serina, her husband

(July 14, 1485) Vt 17, T 8, Ve 16

Peter Serina was a local Brescian businessman to whom Cereta was married at the age of fifteen in December 1484 or January 1485. This is the first of four extant letters to him (for others, see below, 5, 11 and 44). Since she wrote to him in Latin, he must have had an education similar to hers, though as she hints in this letter, hers was better. Her letters were written to him while he was away on business trips to Venice and perhaps other cities. The couple were apparently separated a good deal even during their short marriage. He died from the plague after they had been married only eighteen months. This event, the central one during the years her letters were composed, is one of the chief factors enabling us to date the letters as precisely as we can. The letter fills just over one printed page.

Summary. Cereta expresses her anguish that her husband has not written her and wonders whether he is passing some judgment on her by his silence. She professes her innocence, whatever the charge. ❧

4. *To Benedict Arsagus, Papiensi*

(July 20, 1485) Vt 5, Ve 4

For text, see below, II. The recipient of this letter is unknown to me from other sources.

Summary. No one should boast of wisdom but, impelled by a desire for immortality, of industriousness. She writes because knowledge should be shared and because she seeks to immortalize her name. ❧

5. *To Peter Serina, her husband*

(July 22, 1485) Vt 19, T 10, Ve 18

On her husband; see above, 3.

Summary. Her husband chastised her for not writing but then, when she did write, condemned her for speaking impulsively. She is distressed to the point of tears, even as she had been by his departure for Venice. ❧

6. *To Benedict Arsagus, Papiensi*

(July 24, 1485) Vt 6, Ve 5

For text, see below,III. This is the second of two letters to this correspondent (see above, 4).

Summary. She refers to one elegant letter written to her by this correspondent in both Greek and Latin. She attempts to match his eloquence with a rhetoric of her own in which his writing is compared with flowers on the riverbanks of Helicon and the meadows of Parnassus. You are hastening to fame, she concludes, on the horse of Bellerophon [Pegasus]. ❧

7. *To John Olivieri, Grammarian*
(August 1, 1485) Vt 46, T 39, Ve 41

This is the first of a number of letters addressed to John Olivieri, a grammarian (see below, 38, 39, 45, and 70). Olivieri was a well-known teacher in the province of Brescia during his day. Born around 1444 in Chiari, he completed his studies there and married Helena of an old Chiari family. He returned to Chiari to teach in 1487 after an absence of a few years and remained there until his death in 1497 (his wife died before him in 1493; Cereta mentions a significant visit from her, see below, 70). He taught a number of noblemen who in turn became men of learning, and he himself received a title of nobility before he died. He left no works. These and other details of his biography may be found in Ludovico Ricci, "Notizie di Giovanni Olivieri," *Nuova raccolta d'opuscoli scientifici e filologici* (Venezia: Simone Occhi, 1770), Vol. 20, opus. 6, pp. 3–18. In his discussion of some of Olivieri's pupils, Ricci does not mention the Cereta brothers commended to him by Cereta in this letter (Hippolytus and Basil) and in letter 39, below (Basil and Daniel). The letter fills almost two printed pages.

It is curious that Cereta rather than her father should have written this letter. Perhaps she was only assisting him in the matter or simply demonstrating to the future teacher of her brothers that there were already members in the Cereta household well educated in the disciplines he taught. Of course, the situation also reflects the fact that Olivieri's school was for boys only. Cereta could receive the kind of education Olivieri provided only if she could get it at home.

Summary. She sends greetings to his wife and thanks her for having been gracious to them before [indicating that this is not the beginning of a relationship between the two families]. She then commends to him two of her brothers, Hippolytus and Basil, as worthy pupils who need the instruction and discipline which a good teacher can provide. Their father, as well as the rest of the family, hope that they will also enjoy their learning at his hands. She assures him that the boys will love him all the more if he can instill in them a love for good literature. Success with them will redound to his own glory. ❧

wretched state of mind which affects her writing. Yet she writes to Albert anyway, not only because she feels obligated to him like a daughter, but equally because she knows that he will not judge her harshly for the lack of eloquence her writing is bound to display. ❧

59. To Frontonus Carito
(July 1, 1487) Vt 58, T 50, Ve 53

This is the only letter to this correspondent, who is unknown to me from other sources. He may be addressed here as "Dear Frontonus." The letter is just over one printed page.

Summary. Frontonus had written to her that Eusebius read her letters and judged them to be written not by her but by her father [see below, 63]. She is honored by this charge, for she regards her father as the best of writers. Moreover, he taught her all she knows in her younger years. On the other hand, Eusebius is no more trustworthy in this matter than Orosius, whose learning has real limitations and no subtlety. He is quite envious of her. Still, she wonders where this charge came from, since she has been absent from her father for a long time. In any case, she gives thanks to these detractors who exalt the father's knowledge rather than the daughter's ignorance. ❧

60. Invective against Orestes and Phronicus
(July 1, 1487) Vt 73, T 61, Ve 63

This is the only letter addressed to either of these correspondents, who are unknown to me from other sources. Both, however, are mentioned again in 63, below and Phronicus also in 74, below. The criticism to which, in an explosion of fury, Cereta responds here, is that to which she alludes in the letter to her father (above, 30) as well as in the letter immediately preceding this one. The force of her response suggests that we have in the published correspondence only a small part of what must have passed back and forth. The invective fills eight printed pages.

Summary. She has received their illiterate babbling letters. She marvels that Orestes should dare to do combat with her, for she remembers that when they were children he was a poor learner, interested more in his stomach than in his mind. Indeed, people would question him about his stomach god. His speech was barbaric and his gestures and inflections nonsensical. Many at the time wrote derisory things about him. She chides him that while he believed his criticisms would discredit her, they have rather caused her to be accepted in circles where before she was unknown. Even so, did he think she would be passive and silent forever? He should cease saying that, although she does not lack zeal, she is ignorant in literature. For he has not put forward any word of his own—apart from his criticism of her—which could be either praised or blamed. He and Phronicus have emerged, as it were, out of the latrine of infamy, as if gathered from the stinking foam of the lower world. They are both excluded from the senate of letters like the cadaver of a putrid beast. They wield clubs rather than speech, to which silence would be preferable. One is known by his speech. Moreover, as one speaks, so will he be spoken to. They have said that Cereta left the goddesses of poetry sad and hungry on Parnassus and has sung not of heroes or gods but has recounted the well-known tales told in barber shops. Oh sly monster! Oh dirt! Oh filth! she cries. By such an accusation as this, does an ape become a Ciceronian? Thersites [a Greek noted for his filthy tongue] has nothing to do with Lycurgus [Athenian orator famed for his integrity]. A strong tendency to envy is always the distinguishing mark of an infamous person. ❧

61. To Alphonse Tiburtinus

(July 20, 1487) Vt 57, T 49, Ve 52

This is the only letter to this correspondent, who is unknown to me from other sources. The letter fills less than two printed pages.

Summary. His letters have aroused her indignation and hurt her feelings, especially the news that Lucretia believes there can be no equality of the sexes so far as learning and intellect are concerned. Cereta does not know what would be an acceptable response to such a belief. She is afraid that she has said something to kindle envy—which is obviously behind Lucretia's remark. But she has always honored Lucretia and has never spoken ill of her. If Lucretia knows something Cereta does not know, she should tell Cereta. A good person does not make vague charges and then withdraw. She asks Alphonse to keep her informed about these rumors. ❧

62. To Veneranda, Abbottess of St. Chiara
(August 13, 1487) Vt 55, T 48, Ve 50

This is the only letter addressed to this correspondent who is unknown to me from other sources. The letter fills less than two printed pages.

Summary. Cereta congratulates Veneranda for having been chosen head of a convent. She proposes to prepare Veneranda for the account she must give to God. She should remember that all those to whom God has given kingdoms to rule have returned the kingdoms to him, whether Solomon and David or Pharaoh and Nebuchadnezzar. She should remember as well that others—Jeremiah and Saul among Christians and Lycurgus, Empedocles, Pittacus and Lycophron among the pagans—refused the kingdoms offered them or laid aside their possessions voluntarily. Veneranda should so judge those under her that she anticipates disturbances and avoids the necessity of judgment. Remember that all are judged after death, that this life itself is a shadow, and that our desires are disappointed. Remember that every moment we exist is owed to the grace of God. Let her see to it that the high altar is not polluted by a domineering spirit. Consider to what misery we can be led by death and so live that death will lead to happiness. ❧

63. To Boniface Bembo or Lorenzo Capreolo
(August 22, 1487) Vt 66, T 53, Ve 55

In Vt this letter is addressed to Boniface Bembo (see above, 10) but in T and Ve to Lorenzo Capreola who is addressed nowhere else in the correspondence and who is unknown to me from other soures. The letter may well have been copied in two versions. In Vt the person mentioned several times as criticizing Cereta is Cassandra Fedele (see above, 55), and Venice is mentioned as the place to which the case may be referred, but in T and Ve the person criticizing her is Gismunda (whose name uniformly replaces that of Cassandra) and reference is made to Rome as the place to which the case may be referred. Moreover, in T (but not in Ve) there is one place where the name of

Boniface, who is addressed directly in the passage, is retained, suggesting that the letter was indeed originally written to him and then subsequently adapted by change of names to a second correspondent, though in one place the changes were not consistently carried out. Since it is known that Boniface did not go to Rome until 1493, I would guess that the letter as it is contained in Vt is the original letter, written in 1487, and that this same letter was copied with the changes mentioned into the other manuscripts at a later date. This supports the view that Vt is not only our only complete source but is also the oldest, even if it cannot be demonstrated to be the archetype.

The letter fills over four printed pages.

Summary. Cassandra has accused her but without bringing forth any charges. She thus seems stimulated by a strong impulse to rivalry. It seems that she has contempt for her equals or wishes to increase suspicion of those who are perhaps more knowledgeable than herself. Cereta protests that her goodness does not merit her being accused of a false knowledge. It would be better to flatter someone than to treat them in this way. She is afraid Boniface may believe all that Cassandra says. No one should make accusations against another in the other's absence. No judge would admit evidence without a charge and proof of the charge. Cassandra believes that it was not Cereta but Cereta's father who wrote her letters [see above, 59]. Cereta professes astonishment that with no evidence at all she should make such an assertion. After all, she and Cassandra are both of the same age and sex, even if in learning Cassandra is more advanced. Cassandra is not the only one who has said such things, however. Phronicus, Orestes, and Eusebius have accused her of having a rustic pen [see above, 60]. But look at the evidence. She has, after all, written to a number of outstanding people. Therefore, Boniface should not believe the charges against her. If reason is the judge then she is innocent. Indeed, she considers the charges beneath her and reaffirms her innocence. Cassandra should consider herself justifiably admonished by a sister and recognize that Cereta has spoken because she felt compelled to do so and for the sake of clarity.

64. *To Albert de Albertis*
(August 23, 1487) Vt 52, T 45, Ve 47

See above, 8. The letter fills over two printed pages.

Summary. She is appreciative of his exhortations during her period of greatest sorrow, which helped her overcome her despair. She announces that she is putting aside her apathy and taking up her studies once again. She hopes in the future to glorify his name, though she believes he must await better poets and orators than she is to be made illustrious. She professes great respect for his learning but even more for his virtue. She asks him not to be contemptuous of her efforts, for while others may be found who are more talented, no one is more diligent. If everything is not perfectly said, perhaps, nonetheless, things will be said well enough that those now living and still to come will love and admire him. ❧

65. *To Louis Dandalus, Magistrate of Brescia*
(August 29, 1487) Vt 51, T 44, Ve 46

This is the only letter to this correspondent, who is unknown to me from other sources. The letter is an oration with the title "On the German Conflict." For a discussion of it, see above, the section on the dating of extant materials. The oration fills over five printed pages.

Summary. The Germans came and beseiged and blockaded the straits of Italy, then, while they were winning, withdrew to Germany. Why they did so no one can say; if there were military motives they are unknown to a young girl. Perhaps they dissipated their animosity or satisfied their sense of justice. Perhaps they were ashamed that Christians were fighting against Christians and that so many people were being killed and so many fields laid waste. But whether sent back by our people or their own, they have returned to their own country. May they long remain there. All of Italy is now completely at rest, which has never been enough the case.

When the Germans first attacked they could not take the city and fled. They were pursued by the Italians, who were in turn ambushed by fresh German forces waiting in the woods in the path of their retreat. There was fierce fighting near the Adige River [near Brescia]. Throwing a bridge across the river, the Italians attacked with cavalry. But the bridge collapsed, demoralizing the soldiers and stirring the Germans to counterattack. Many Italian soldiers perished in the water or on the side of the river on which they had been stranded. But battle only induces the winner to more battle, so that war and destruction generate more war and destruction. Brescia should have followed Venice in building fortifications that were unconquerable. Indeed the Venetians not only can repel assault but can punish the offenders by laying waste provinces and sea coasts with their fleets. Honor belongs to such a country. •

66. *To Clement Longulus, Grammarian*

(October 1, 1487) Vt 44, T 37, Ve 39

See above, 23. This letter fills less than two printed pages.

Summary. Many at Chiara [see above, 30] wrote to her shortly after she began going there. Only Clement rejected her; she protests his injustice in doing so. She does not know him by sight but only by reputation. She wrote to him earlier [see above, 23] and cannot understand his anger. He regards her as of no value, even though others value her. Instead of writing to her, he has brought accusations against her. She would prefer—and would welcome—letters from him. For the liberal arts demonstrate virtue and display the fruits of labor which lead to immortality. Although she is occupied with many things that concern women, she still writes to turn him away from his anger and to ask him to reconsider their relationship. ❧

67. *To Martha Marcella*

(October 8, 1487) Vt 70, T 58, Ve 60

This is the only letter to this correspondent, who is unknown to me from other sources. The letter is an oration, filling about eight printed pages, which bears the title "Consolation on the Death of her Husband."

The letter has two parts, the first describing her own earlier attitude toward her husband's death, including a partial retelling of her dream of a voyage to the underworld (see above, 55) and the second exhorting her friend in various ways to adopt a proper attitude toward death.

Summary. If we could fly to the lower world, perhaps we could have commerce with the best of men, Peter and Laelius. But in vain do we seek admission. Cereta recalls an earlier dream in which she was taken through the flames of Phlegethon and muddy Acheron, and saw the Tartarean powers with her own eyes. She confesses, however, that in all this she was deceived. She was suffering from despair at the loss of her husband. It was in this state of mind that she saw Charon striking souls with an oar, the dog Cerberus exposing other souls to more monstrous beasts, people being thrown over cliffs. These bitter visions finally left her and she conceived a more certain hope that on the day of judgment she would meet her husband just as he is, for his constancy in life kept him out of the lower world after death.

She exhorts Martha not to lose herself in tears or tear out her hair. Rather should she remember that there is nothing greater than the soul. Even if he were the best of men, he could not avoid death of the body, though his spirit will live forever. Epicurus teaches us that wisdom can be content with itself, that virtue is sweeter than any friend, and that our happiness proceeds from virtue rather than from wealth or from a husband [see below, 76]. It is enough that we have honored our husbands by mourning. We should not, in addition, be frightened by the caprice of fortune to such an extent that our souls are troubled. They lived an ordered life, and God is not unjust. That should fill us with tranquillity. The ways to death are many, but the occurrence itself is uncertain as to time for each of us. We should so live that we may rise above it when it strikes those we love. ❧

68. From Brother Thomas of Milan to Silvester Cereta
(October 9, 1487) Vt 59

For text, see below,IX. This is the first of four letters written by Brother Thomas, the only letters in Cereta's collection not written by Cereta herself. The present letter is the only one in the corpus not written by or to Cereta. On Brother Thomas, see above, 49. This letter is dated October 9, 1487 and is one of only two letters in the entire corpus which bears a year date. The other is 39 above.

Summary. Neither a miser nor a liberal man is ever satisfied with the wealth he has. So also the soul, which strives toward heaven, is never satisfied inasmuch as it is weak and always wants more than it can obtain. With this analogy Brother Thomas says that Silvester has aroused his desire by sending him Cereta's letters, and he knows that the desire, now that it is aroused, will not grow faint again. Reading her letters has excited him. Her letter to Felix Tadinus [see above, 57], for example, moves him with its assertion that her wound [the death of her husband] was not healed by crying but by reason. Her letter to Sigismund shows great skill in its organization and eloquence [see above, 29]. Her account of the battle at the Adige River [35], her description of the foolish display of ornamented women [54], her investigations of the heavens [24, 38, 39] and of plants [21], her dream of going to the underworld [55], reveal the fertility of her mind. What has remained unknown to this girl? What has nature kept hidden from her? But the letters lead him to more internal reflection.

In all the learning of this age, there has been a great neglect of holy things. Christ does not today dwell among us. There is no Ambrose, Antony, or Augustine. They would dwell with us daily if we read their books. Rarely, however, do we contemplate them. If we love them, we should imitate them. He asks both Laura and Silvester to be patient with him, for he is consumed by zeal for God. He closes with the pious hope that Laura will always be strengthened and comforted in God's strength. ❧

69. A Poem
appended to Vt 59

For text, see below,IX. This poem appears in Vt immediately following 69 above. It has no heading. There is no indication that Cereta wrote it, and since it is appended to a letter by Brother Thomas, contains a veiled reference to Cereta, and is later referred to by Brother Thomas in a letter to Cereta (see below,XII: 195 ff.), it was doubtless written by him. Insofar as the poem is related to the corpus of letters and is not simply an exercise or display of poetic virtuosity, it appears to refer to Cereta the controversialist who will be destroyed by her harsh exchanges of letters with critics. In this respect, the poem anticipates many of the things Brother Thomas will say in subsequent letters to Cereta herself.

The form of the poem is strange. It is surrealistic, as if recounting a dream or conjuring up one (see above, 55). It fills twenty lines.

Summary. The poem opens with a description of a deep slumber out of which comes a dream of an approaching ship with a tall mast. Cereta is the mast. A storm arises and the ship is sunk in a whirlpool. The dreamer shudders and hears a voice tell him to pluck the laurel. ❧

70. To John Olivieri
(October 31, 1487) Vt 45, T 38, Ve 40

See above, 7. The letter fills less than two printed pages.

Summary. She comments on Olivieri's surprise that she has written letters to him in a polished Latin. Olivieri's wife has come and asked for a letter on the spot. Cereta is obliging her with this one, though she suspects he is probing the extent of her education. She has been taught by her father, from whom she has gotten a great deal, but she has graduated from his tutelage and does what she does independently. Perhaps, she says, she will rise higher than Ida [a mountain in Crete where Zeus was nourished]. But let the argument not become too serious. Youth should be judged by what it can do. She closes with the promise to say more about this at another time. ❧

71. To Lucilia Vernacula
(November 1, 1487) Vt 67, T 54, Ve 56

This is the only letter to this correspondent, who is unknown to me from other sources. The letter is a brief oration (filling over two printed pages) with the title "Against Women who disparage Learned Women." It is one among the letters (see below, 77) in which Cereta shows herself the most aggressive of the women of her century in defending learning for her sex.

Summary. Envy has so aroused some women that they deny that any woman can be eloquent in Latin. The wretched men might be forgiven for such madness. But it is impossible to put up with babbling women, who, with their chatter, injure not only their sex but also themselves. Strong only in their ability to gossip, they seek to destroy learned women with their envious poison. Cereta wonders why she should put up with them when noble women express admiration for her. She will not sit quietly and take abuse, for the best should not be allowed to be injured by the worst. Rather should those in solent women be silenced. They cannot bear to hear the name of a learned woman, even though with effort they could easily obtain the learning of which they are envious. Learning is not obtained by a last will and testament or by chance, but by our own effort. If these women choose to spend their time in aimless pleasures they cannot also be learned. Only those gain praise for themselves who study hard and consistently. ❧

72. From Brother Thomas to Laura Cereta
(November 4, 1487) Vt 61

For text, see below, X. On Brother Thomas, see above, 49.

Summary. He accuses Cereta of having hidden a critique of him behind her comments about Boniface. Although Cereta claimed to have found no force in his arguments, Brother Thomas senses otherwise. He is puzzled at what Cereta could have read in his letter that aroused her to treat him so inhumanely, even to the point of calling him irrational. At the same time, Cereta sends her own work to all the learned as if she feared no reproach. While she proclaims humility she seeks renown, certainly a refined form of hypocrisy. Humility is worthless if it rages against everyone who brings an accusation. He urges her to be more level-headed, curtail the sharpness of her language, and dull her pen. Let her remember the significance of her name: poison avoids laurel berries and is dissolved by laurel. ❧

73. To Brother Thomas of Milan
(November 11, 1487) Vt 62, T 56, Ve 58

See above, 49. The letter fills three printed pages. It is clearly a response (at least in part) to 72 above, to which it explicitly refers once.

Summary. His letter has angered her, because it raises so many painful thoughts. But she is not guilty as accused by him. If Plato rejected Parmenides and Socrates Anaxagoras, if Diogenes rejected Euclid and Cicero Mark Antony, what is all that to her [references to a lost letter of Brother Thomas?]? Rather does she rejoice that the name of Laura has made everyone envious. The fact that her writings are displeasing to the common crowd is proof of her integrity. She knows that she pays more heed to the imminence of death than to her reputation. He should not believe that she has attacked him, for she honors him as a philosopher. Moreover, she would have him know that she has renounced the world and determined that nothing shall be pleasing to her except what is permitted. Her mind is set on death and focused on her savior. And since this is the case, she is particularly bothered by his accusations. She is hungry for study and literature, but not because she seeks glory. If further defense is needed, she will explain herself in a humble little room with Christ. Paralogisms and definitions she will leave to him [see above, 72]. Her defense hereafter will be silence, and patience will be her happiness. Like Ulysses she can bypass the poison songs of the Sirens and sail a true course. Reason can always conquer passions which crawl up from below, so long as virtue rather than pleasure is one's guide. ❧

74. From Brother Thomas of Milan to Laura Cereta
(November 25, 1487) Vt 63

For text, see below, XI. On Brother Thomas, see above, 49.

Summary. He likens the arrival of her letter to that of an angry swarm of honey bees. She ascribes to him opinions he does not hold and accuses him of an anger he does not have. He does not wish to match her anger but rather to tame it. Did he not praise her writings in his recent letter to Silvester? [See above, 68]. Why is she angry that he said the controversies in which she was engaged are unworthy of her? He still thinks Phronicus is possessed of an imperial will and is in partnership with magpies and peacocks [see above, 60]. But he is astounded at her hostility to him. He has not turned against her as have Eusebius and Cassandra [see above, 59 and 63]. Rather has he praised her virtue and regards her as an unusual young person inasmuch as she lives a celibate life and continues her studies amid the pressing duties of domestic life. If he sees a spot or wrinkle, she should remember that nothing earthly is perfect.

She should listen to the warnings of one who loves her. Oratory seeks a platform and public commendation. The orator, like a peacock, wants to impress. He struts about looking distinguished and raises the expectations of the rustic crowd that surrounds him. Gesturing with his hands and-wrinkling his eyebrows, he speaks foolishness, thinking all the while that he is transforming himself from a nobody into Ptolemy or Cato or Pliny. So also in her oration in honor of an ass [see above, 1], she recounts his life. In doing so she exposed herself as a fraud. [Brother Thomas appears to lack a sense of humor.] We are really said to understand something when we know the causes and see clearly the truth of the deduced conclusions. But nothing ever really falls into this category. We therefore should not think about things whose causes are unknown and from which all kinds of conclusions can be drawn. One who does not spend the time of his study in vain knows that he knows nothing and does not pursue such knowledge. Those, on the other hand, who do not know that they know nothing, think they are something great.

Humility is the greatest ornament. A spiritual person like the Virgin Mary never looks down or back but keeps her eyes fixed on God. Therefore, Cereta should restrain her missiles until she has dipped them in the blood of love. Love is patient and kind and always supportive. It rejoices in the truth.

Cereta professes to rejoice that her writings have made everyone envious [see above, 73]. Does she include him in the "everyone"? He does not include himself. She seems to regard him as one of the villianous who seeks fame by destroying others. Thus Herostratus sought fame by burning the Temple of Lucina on the night Alexander the Great was born. Nero is famous as a monstrous beast, for he killed his mother Agrippina who had herself killed Claudius with a mushroom. In inflating Cereta's glory he did not wish to injure his own name.

He confesses that he is not her equal in skill or talent, but neither is he in acrimony. She is like a careless chess player who allows her most important pieces to be captured and is finally checkmated by a pawn. She should remember that the charges she brings against others will often be turned back against her. In any case, he has been wounded by her abusiveness and desires peace. He closes, however, with the fear that this letter will only make her more angry. ❧

75. From Brother Thomas to Laura Cereta
(December 12, 1487) Vt 65

For text, see below, XII. On Brother Thomas, see above, 49. See also 78, below, for the relation of this letter to that one.

Summary. Her oratory is inflammatory and makes him feel as if all eyes are turned on him. But why should she pursue him so, since he has not exalted himself and, indeed, has praised her? He recognizes that he lacks the kind of learning she has. He has never read an oration of Cicero's, though he has studied Seneca and Lucan. But even these he was unable to pursue for long. Nevertheless, he attempts to imitate her as best he can.

But she has overrated herself to the point of thinking that even the best thinkers of the past are unworthy of her esteem, although in relation to them she is nothing. Thus, he says, he mocks her even as she mocks him. The Lord teaches us that we should be humble and so we should. Today, however, anger, impatience, and cruelty are called courage, pride is called generosity of mind, and ambition is honored as splendor and clarity. On the other, goodness, kindness, gentleness, humility, patience, and piety which are the ornaments of a true humanity, are thought to belong to the lazy and stupid. Some say that man is the noblest of creatures, limited by no order [cf. Pico della Mirandola]. But even the lowest heavenly creatures surpass humans. Even, however, if one admits that man is the noblest of created beings, it is still true that the gold is mixed with dross. Is not the human body so weak that even a filthy gnat can disquiet or kill it? As body alone, man is the vilest among vile creatures. But even his immaterial aspect, as noted, is assigned a lowly place among incorporeal beings.

God hates pride. As she has said in her letters, death threatens us at all times. Only he is meritorious who is always mindful of death. For one who cannot face death cannot face life either. Death releases the good soul from the burden of the body, ends its exile, and returns it to its rightful home. But those who so live that they perpetuate the work of death in life will die a bitter death, inasmuch as they will be eternally punished. He therefore exhorts her to act as though she were the companion of John Cassian. Thus will she assure herself of being received into the highest heaven as one approved by the Lord. She knows what kind of person God desires her to become. God imparts every good to each according to the merits he is capable of achieving. If God completes what he began in her, she will experience His grace from the present and eternally. ❧

76. *To her sister Deodata di Leno, a Nun*
(December 12, 1487) Vt 75, T 63, Ve 65

This is the only letter to this sister. She wrote one to her other sister, Diana (see above, 41). This letter bears the title "Topography and Defense of Epicurus" and fills nine printed pages.

The letter is almost equally divided into two parts, the first of which describes a physical journey, whether intended literally or metaphorically is not clear, and the second of which describes a spiritual journey.

Summary. Cereta proposes to respond to her sister's question regarding how one ought to journey through life and then to defend Epicurus, whose idea of pleasure her sister had attacked.

Cereta describes a journey by sea which brings her party to a valley surrounded by mountains. They disembarked and began to ascend one of the mountains. They satisfied their hunger as they went by picking wild fruit. They circled around the mountain, finally arriving at the top. After a pleasant rest they started down again. They found themselves in a thick wood and at length reached a river, whose course they followed. Emerging finally from the woods, they arrived at a home which had been their destination and enjoyed a feast of nuts and fruits, foods eaten with bread and wine.

But the austerity of Socrates is preferable to the gluttony of Sardanapalus. Only the miserable give themselves to pleasures. Since this is so, she urges her sister to journey with her mind, seeking not the tranquillity of mountain tops but of her soul. For this journey virtue is necessary. [See on this physical/metaphorical journey, Petrarch's *Ascent of Mont Ventoux*.]

This leads into her defense of Epicurus. He was a temperate man who counseled moderation, and not out of fear. He judged that pleasure greatest which came from freedom of mind, for only a contented soul, as opposed to one living in fear of punishment, could achieve happiness. Christians have their hearts filled with the love of God (and therefore are the true Epicureans). But our souls are housed in weak flesh as beings in exile. This, however, is the price of paradise.

She urges that both she and her sister keep their attention focused on the Savior and imitate the illustrious figures from the Christian past who longed for eternal life. To do this, they should look upon every day as if it were the last, so that they may be kept happy in the midst of the quicksand of life and be brought at last to God, the highest enjoyment.

She closes by urging her sister to write her often, for her letters make her seem present. ❧

77. To Bibulus Sempronius
(January 13, 1488) Vt 77, T 65, Ve 67

This is the only letter to this correspondent who is unknown to me from other sources. The letter is one of the most vigorous defenses of women in relation to learning penned in the fifteenth century, or, indeed, in any age. It carries the title "Defense of the Liberal Instruction of Women" and fills eight printed pages.

The letter is divided into three parts. The first attacks the correspondent directly for his attitude toward Cereta in particular and women in general. The second part cites many examples from classical sources of the deeds of outstanding women, some taken from history, some from mythology. The last section discusses the reasons why the sexes are different intellectually and what conduces to their being the same.

Summary. He has praised her as a learned woman but in doing so has singled her out as if she were unique. Such adulation is a deception, for it expresses, in an indirect way, contempt of women in general. She will show him, however, that there have been learned women in every age.

There have been a number of women prophetesses or soothsayers, e.g., the Ethiopian Sabba, who was asked to come and sing her oracles not far from Baiae [on the coast of Campania]. Sibyl sold books of oracles to Tarquinius [king of Rome]. The Babylonian prophetess Heriphyle prophesied the fall of Troy, the fortunes of the Roman Empire, and the coming of Christ. The Egyptian Zenobia taught letters not only to the Egyptians but also to the Greeks and Romans. Athena taught many arts to the Athenians. The Lesbian Sappho sang verses which seem to have come from the lyre of Orpheus or Apollo. Proba had an outstanding knowledge of both Greek and Latin and used it to write biblical stories in Vergilian verse. Among other ancient figures, Sempronia was a powerful Roman poet and orator, Hortensia [daughter of Hortensius] was celebrated for her eloquence, as were Cornificia Germana [daughter of the poet Cornificius] and Tulliola [daughter of Cicero]. To these ancients can be added our contemporaries Niculosa of Bologna,

Isotta Nogarola, and Cassandra Fedele. Given all these examples, he should admit that nature is impartial in the distribution of its gifts.

Still, she admits that learning in women is more rare than in men, and she asks why this is the case. Custom, she responds, accounts for the difference. Many women are taught to be concerned only about their bodies. Those who aspire to greater things must discipline their bodies so that they may train their minds. For knowledge is no gift; it results only from study. Unfortunately, women are not encouraged to study.

She therefore rejects his praise, because it is given under the guise of contempt for women. Moreover, her own accomplishments are small, so that his praise of her appears doubly satirical and contemptuous of women. She wants none of the kind of protection *he* would give to women. Rather does she prefer to defend women herself and attack chatterboxes and empty noisemakers who heap abuse upon women. ❧

78. *To Brother Thomas of Milan*
(Feb. 4, 1488) Vt 64, T 71, Ve 73

See above, 49. There is a conflict among the sources in dating this letter. Ve and T agree on a date of February 4, [1488], while Vt dates the letter December 11, [1487]. The letter belongs after the last letter of Brother Thomas to Cereta (75, above), for she alludes to his reference to John Cassian in that letter. Since the latter is dated December 12 [1487], a date of December 11 [1487] for this letter is impossible.

Brother Thomas is addressed here as "Philosopher of the Order of Preachers." The letter fills about six printed pages.

Summary. She says she is responding to several of his previous letters in this one. She compliments him for his eloquence, style, and understanding. She commends him for having avoided the sophisms of the dialecticians while at the same time being at home in Aristotle. This has been conducive to clearing up many enigmas.

She commends him also for serving religion above all else. He has shown a humility and absence of ambition commensurate with his monasticism. He has shown that he is ready for death and that his home is not in this world.

She is impressed with the examples he has given her of those who have shown their faith by sequestering themselves from the world. From his examples she has learned that the body is inferior to the soul and that the conscience is the seat of the soul. Having learned this she has decided to turn away from letters; she does not want her mind diverted by vain and transitory things. Although study is not to be despised, we were not born for literature alone. Indeed, God prefers an innocent heart to a learned mind. Moreover, the death of her husband makes death as desirable to her as life.

She has therefore decided to place herself in his hands for guidance. She thanks him especially because he has lifted from her the burden of writing. Thus she is bringing to a close this first part of her familiar letters [in saying so, she implies that there are other parts and that this is the last letter in the first part—see below, 84]. What remains for her now is to find a higher way. Reflecting on possible courses of action she says that perhaps she will undertake the study of higher things [religion?] or simply live a more relaxed leisurely life. She will not, she adds, be able to refrain from work altogether, but her work need not suffer because she also rests. ❧

79. To Bernard Laurinus, Grammarian

(February 13, 1488) Vt 78, T 66, Ve 68

This is the only letter to this correspondent, who is otherwise unknown to me. The letter fills less than four printed pages.

Summary. Even though the death of her husband has enervated her, she wants to respond to poems and letters he has sent to her. She describes for him how she responded to her husband's death. After her initial despair she took refuge in religion. But then she turned to a love of study and literature and through this means overcame her grief. Others also have overcome misfortune. She cites classical figures (Ulysses, Scipio, Hannibal) as well as Christians (Faustinus, Jovita, Vincent, Stephen) to illustrate her point. A healthy mind never rests until it is ordered.

Some sadness must necessarily accompany our earthly existence. We overcome this by turning from human to universal things, by concerning ourselves with knowledge and virtue alone. She asserts that a new vigor is growing within her, but one which seeks chaste opinions and sacred law rather than eloquence.

He has praised Cassandra Fedele to her. But no one knows Cassandra's qualities better than she does. She, in fact, wrote to Cassandra about an imaginary visit to the underworld [see above, 55], as well as other letters [not extant]. She invites him to compare this letter of hers with Cassandra's work, asking him not to make premature judgments. ❧

80. To Marius Bonus

(February 26, 1487/1488) Vt 80, T 68, Ve 70

This is the only letter to this correspondent, who is unknown to me from other sources. The letter is entitled "On Waiting upon an Apparition" and fills about two printed pages.

Summary. She is writing in the evening after having seen an apparition in the afternoon. She was conversing with a group of women when all of them saw an apparition of someone half naked holding a serpent tightly in its left hand and dancing in public without shame. When they saw it they were frightened and retreated. In retaliation, the creature threatened punishment against them, shouting filthy obscenities against everyone. Then it vanished before their eyes. Everyone was amazed.

If this thing was a man, how did it get out of its heavy body into the air? If it was a spirit, from what pit or by what command of God did it emerge? It was not any Sisyphus, Orestes, Tantalus, or Ascalaphus among men. And it did not come from the fatal abode of Pluto where the snaky-haired Eumenides or the dreadful Gorgons and Cerberus live. Nor had it the appearance of the Furies.

What these dreadful portents reveal she does not understand, but she was certainly frightened by the appearance and its possible meanings. ❧

81. To Solitaria Europa

(February 29, 1487/1488) Vt 82, T 70, Ve 72

This is the only letter to this correspondent, who is unknown to me from other sources. The letter is entitled "Admonition on the False Delights of a Solitary Life." The name of the person to whom the letter is addressed in relation to the content of the letter suggests the possibility that this may be a letter not to another person but to herself (cf. the first part of her letter to her sister Deodata, 76, above). This would make it among the earliest soliloquies in the western literary tradition. I owe this suggestion to Professor Richard Harrier of New York University. The letter fills about seven printed pages.

Summary. She has received a letter from Solitaria describing long sojourns in the country. Though delighted by the description, she feels compelled to counter the possible self-deception in the leisure described. Only wisdom, she counters, allows us to escape the helplessness of babies, the ignorance of girls, and the ugliness, boredom, and misery of old age. Such wisdom is not achieved in solitude but in remaining constant through the evils which accompany life.

Solitaria wanders about mountains, listens to the singing of nightingales, finds peace on the banks of the Mella River [near Brescia]. Cereta does not deny that the area is beautiful with its thick forests, brooks teeming with fish, wild game, and fruits and nuts which may be gathered at random. But Solitaria is led astray by all this. She believes she is emulating famous Romans, like Camillus, the Curios, Metullus, P. Scipio, Q. Cincinnatus, and Sylla, or famous Greeks like Pittacus, Anaxagoras, Euripides, Mysones, Heraclitus, and Parmenides. All of those named preferred a pastoral setting to the delights of the cities, as more conducive to a tranquil life. But none of them expected another life after death. Solitaria, on the other hand, has been baptized a Christian and should find a solace commensurate with her Christianity. Otherwise she is no different from pagans who cultivated Pan, Silvanus and other gods of the woods. It is true that many philosophers have sprung from such places. But they are not to be compared to Christian souls whose humility and innocence brought them to the eternal hierarchies of the blessed. *This* is the happiness Christians seek; happiness of life on earth has always been foreign to Christianity.

Solitaria, therefore, should rethink her choice of a solitary life. A life which accepts the disturbances of the present world is the best preparation for life after death. Thus she should not avoid but admit the anguish of widows and young bereaved persons. Her own approaching death will trouble her less if she does so. She should so act that when death comes, it will not find her unprepared. ❧

82. To Lupus Cynicus
(March 1, 1487/1488) Vt 79, T 67, Ve 69

This is the only letter to this correspondent, who is otherwise unknown to me. The letter is an oration and is entitled "Warning against Avarice." It fills over five printed pages.

Summary. Why, she asks, does Cynicus so love money? His excess is not in *what* he accumulates but in the *anxiety* that makes him thirst for more. Thus, even if he had all the wealth of India, Asia, and Africa he would not be content. Of what use would it all be anyway, since death will claim everything in the end? Even a very long life does not guarantee happiness. Priam lived to an old age only to see Troy destroyed. Croesus lost his empire to Cyrus when he was an old man. Nor does fame assure happiness. M. Marcellus was drowned at the height of his glory, Julius Caesar was murdered after attaining power, and Alexander the Great died of poison after conquering the world.

We are all implicated in the sin of Adam, and none of us can escape its consequence—death. The monuments people have built for themselves have not survived the ravages of time and death. This is as true of the Pharaohs and Caesars as of the rest of us. But if this is so, why store up wealth?

Since all the wealth in the world will not save you, be better advised and turn to religion so that you may gain in virtue. Virtue will lead to eternal life, for virtue prepares one to meet the death of the body. If what she has said is true, Cynicus will turn away from his desire for wealth and prepare himself through repentance for the journey to heaven. ❧

83. To Cardinal Maria Ascanius Sforza

(February 28, 1488) Vt 83, T 72, Ve 74

This is the epilogue to Cereta's epistles, addressed to the person to whom they are dedicated, as is also the prologue (see below, 84). The letter fills over two printed pages.

Ascanius Maria Sforza was created a Cardinal Deacon of S. Vito on March 17, 1484 by Pope Sixtus IV. He was a friend of Cardinal Rodrigo Borgia whose election as Pope Alexander VI he advanced. In 1493 he performed the marriage of Lucrezia Borgia. In June 1494 he defected from Alexander VI and spoke of deposing him. In December of the same year he accompanied Charles VIII as he passed through Italy. He played a role in the signing of a treaty between the pope and the king and entered Rome with Charles on December 31, 1494. Reconciled to Alexander, he was suspected of complicity in the assassination of the Duke of Gandia, in which the pope had a hand. He left Rome for Milan in 1499 but was captured by the Venetians and turned over to the French. He returned to Rome only on September 10, 1503 for the conclave, with aspirations of becoming pope. At length he supported Cardinal Giuliano della Rovere, who became Pope Julius II. He died in Rome on May 27, 1505 (*Enciclopedia Cattolica* [Firenze: Sansoni, 1953], Vol. XI, 474).

Summary. She is sending him the first fruits of her rustic pen which she had earlier promised. He is worthy of a better gift, but it is the mind of the giver and not the gift which is most important. At first she feared that the verbosity of her letters would make them loathsome to the reader and even discredit the Latin language. But the hope of his forgiveness served as an antidote to her modesty. Thus she sends these letters, however devoid they may be of eloquence.

Everything in the letters is her own. Nothing has been stolen from other writers. She is releasing the letters while she is still so young because of requests from people whose judgment she respects. She might have released them even sooner had she had a worthy enough patron. Now in him she has found one. The renown of his name will lend authority to that of a young girl as yet unknown in the world. She hopes that her work, under his auspices, will become known and that his name, in turn, will be made more famous by this dedication of her work to him. ❧

84. To Cardinal Maria Ascanius Sforza
(March 1488) Vt 1, T Prologue

See above, 83. This is Cereta's prologue, the dedication of her collection of letters. It fills over eight printed pages.

This prologue may be divided into three sections. In the first, Cereta outlines in a general way her intellectual development. In the second, she describes the context that called forth her letters and explains in part their content. In the last, she commends her letters to the Cardinal whose fame and virtue, she hopes, will redound to her own glory through this dedication.

Summary. There was some delay in the development in her of a passion for learning [see above, 50]. But once this desire was awakened it turned toward philosophy, then toward mathematics [astrology] for which she developed a burning desire [see above, 38 and 39]. Finally, she turned to religious literature which dissolved the doubts in her mind and kept her on the path to truth. Her love of sacred literature was combined with a disciplined contemplative life. At the same time, she was not content with self-understanding but also desired fame, and so, against the advice of some of her elders, she began to seek confirmation of her learning from others through writing.

Among her earliest compositions was her funeral oration in honor of an ass [see above, 1]. The oration generated envy among some of her peers and led them to attack her. For a while she bore this patiently. Finally, however, unable to endure the silence any longer, she spoke out against her detractors through letters, and they in turn wrote back. At length wearied by this, she withdrew from such responses and prepared this volume of letters for publication. Their form is more simple than elegant, more concise than elaborate. They reflect the fact that she was endowed with natural gifts for learning and that she applied herself diligently to study. But she does not believe that what she has produced fulfills all the promise of her endowment.

It is for this reason that she commends her letters to him. With his support she can present her letters to the world. His protection will prevent sniping attacks against her. His virtue will bestow virtue upon her efforts. Thus she is giving over her letters to him—letters which she has selected [implying that she wrote many more than she includes in this collection—see above, 78]—so that his renown might bring the greatest honor to her also. And she in turn hopes that through the dedication of her letters to him, people in future generations will sing his praises [see above, 83].

PART THREE

Critical Edition of the Unpublished Materials in the Cereta Corpus

Introduction

In the following critical edition, all spellings have been modernized and made uniform without reference to variants used in the manuscript source(s). For example, *i* has been distinguished from *j* and *u* from *v*. Where appropriate *t* has replaced *c* (*otiosus* for *ociosus*), *c* has replaced *t* (*species* for *speties*), *i* has replaced *y* (*lacrimis* for *lachrymis*), and *h* has been dropped (*caritas* for *charitas*) or added (*harmonicos* for *armonicos*); *coelis* becomes *caelis*, *caeterum ceterum*, *foelices felices*, and *preconia praeconia*; *quom* becomes *cum*; *imo* becomes *immo*; and so on. Punctuation has been used to increase the sense of the text without reference to usage contemporary with the manuscripts. The text has also been separated into paragraphs, and line numbers have been added.

General references to well-known classical persons have not been footnoted, though specific references to their works are noted. Less well-known persons are identified in the notes, as well as less familiar references from classical mythology.

The order of the texts follows neither manuscript source but, like Part Two above, is chronological. Thus the oration is printed first, followed by the eleven unpublished letters. Discussion of the correspondents and the contents of the letters is contained in Part Two to which, in each case, the reader is referred.

The Textual Notes record significant variants only. Obvious orthographical errors, insignificant transpositions of words, and emendations called for by normalization are not recorded. Nor are these signalled in the text itself. Specific emendations of the text are noted in two ways. Square brackets [ ] indicate additions or emendations; daggers († †) indicate deletions.

The Latinity of Cereta and Brother Thomas

by Warren S. Smith, Jr.

In the following discussion, the great majority of examples have been drawn from the eleven letters and the oration in this edition, though Cereta's previously published letters (T) are cited from time to time.

With regard to vocabulary, there is a fondness for feminine adjectives and nouns ending in *-trix: culpatrix, largitrix, cognitrix, refrigeratrix, bellatrix, oratrix, spoliatrix, genetrix, inventrix*. Most of these are either totally unknown or rare in Classical Latin, where their masculine equivalents ending in *-tor* (e.g., *largitor, bellator, orator*) are more common.

There is a greater tendency to use abstract nouns than in Classical Latin. Note especially those ending in *-atio: vectatio, circumcursatio, defamulatio, respiratio, abominatio, recordatio, reparatio, dealbatio, exultatio, culpatio*.

Diminutives are very frequent, a normal tendency in post-Classical Latin. We find nouns *(citherula, armillula, saltatriculus, organula)*, adjectives *(pulchellus, misella, solula, letiocula)*, and even an adverb *(saepicule)*.

Comparatives are often used with positive meaning. It is particularly difficult to accustom oneself to this stylistic feature, because it is not used with any consistency. Adjectives so used are *frequentior, crassior, iratior, securior, laxior, angustior*. (This is probably also the explanation for the curious expression *Dii meliores* = *Dii boni*, used by Cereta in T, p. 26 and echoed by Brother Thomas in XII:111.) Adverbs so used are: *generosius, innixius, attentius, sollertius, profanius*. These are only a few among many examples. When a truly comparative sense is intended, *magis* is sometimes added to make this clear, e.g., *dilectius magis*.

Adverbs ending in *-tim* are common: *cunctim, affatim, ostiatim, raptim, certatim, scaliatim, furtim, gurgitatim, minuatim*, and several evidently coined for comic effect: *formiculatim*, "in an ant-like manner" (I:671) and*dentetentim*, "feeling carefully with the teeth" (I:172).

We find a tendency toward frequentative verbs: *concrepitant* = *concrepant, pavitans* = *pavescens, lusitaremus* = *luderemus, gracitat* = *gracillat, flectitans* = *flectens, lectitasse* = *legisse, latitans* = *latens*.

There is a sprinkling of Italian in Brother Thomas's letters (X:73; XI:270, and apparently in some parts of his description of a bombastic orator, XI:99–100 *frappae*). Both writers use a relatively high number of words borrowed or adapted from the Greek: *paralogus, synderesis (= synesis?), chirographae, ecstasis, phthisica, ephemeridies, empyreum, syncopis (= syncope)*. Many, though not all, of these have some parallel in Classical Latin.

With regard to syntax, adjectives and adverbs are sometimes added rather superfluously to reinforce the meaning of a verb or noun: *stridulo susurro, increpentis lyrae, discula conquestio, personatos clamores, interquiescebant otiosae, surgens aetas . . . adolevit, levem pulverulam, elatam arrogantiam*. All but the last two examples are taken from Cereta's funeral oration, where the tone is generally bombastic and incongruous. Thus we may suppose the device was used there deliberately for comic effect.

Medieval Latin in general is characterized by an increased use of prepositional phrases where the Classical would prefer unqualified datives and ablatives. There is little evidence of this practice in Cereta and Brother Thomas, except that ablatives of agent are twice used in place of the dative in the passive periphrastic: *Non est . . . abs te uno . . . flenda conditio* (I:25–26), and *fuitne . . . refugium hoc tuum a nobis cruciandum?* (I:464–66).

The preposition *sub* is used with an extraordinarily wide range of meanings. In addition to the normal Classical usage with the sense of "under" or "during", we find such phrases as *sub ardenti ultionis cura*, "with an ardent concern for revenge" (I:402); *sub eloquentiae gratia*, "combined with the pleasure of eloquence" (IX:91–92); *sub hac infelicioris vitae molestia contorquentur*, "are tortured by this trouble of an unhappy life"

(XI:80–81); and *clara sub natalium generositate humanitas,* "a humanity enhanced by the excellence of your ancestry" (XI:70–71).

Et is inserted loosely many times, particularly in Brother Thomas's letters, often meaning "even" or also" but not always at a point where there is a clear reason for such emphasis; sometimes it is merely a connective to start off a sentence. *Vel* with no more force than *et,* or with no discernible force at all, is also common.

The writers' styles are studiedly complex and demand close attention from the reader. Nouns, adverbs, participles and their objects are often interwoven in a tight structure: *crura . . . incurvatum bacillo corpus lente regentia* (I:167–69), *ne devoveas obtundentes hoc genus diritates in deos* (I:213). Nominatives introduced late in the sentence may add a surprise twist to the meaning: *cecidi super corpus exanimis* (T, p. 66), *rependens . . . beneficium gratus non est* (XI:32–33). There is often a long separation between subject and verb, or between modifier and noun. In Cereta's letters this device tends to be used skillfully to enhance the meaning or produce a special effect, but in Brother Thomas it occasionally has no discernible purpose and merely seems awkward: *barbaris atrocior feris* (does it mean "fierce barbarians" or "savage beasts"?), *et exorbentibus quoque sanguinem Scythis immanior ac* ipso *denique inexorabilior concrepatus est* Acheronte (emphasis added, IX:66–68), *qui longiore sub hac infelicioris vitae molestia contorquentur* (the two modifiers of *molestia* are awkwardly split up by the preposition, IX:80–81). In XI:66–69 the adjective *pretiosus* is separated from its noun by twenty-two intervening words.

Other devices used to surprise the reader or keep him alert are oxymoron and paradoxical statements. Cereta refers (IV:1–2) to *rivi incendia* and *camino inundanti,* "the fires of a river and a flooding furnace" (unless this is intended as a drastic example of transferred epithet). Brother Thomas mentions (XI:228–29) *splendoris tui obnubilatione,* "the cloud of your brightness." Cereta speaks (T, p. 188) of *oculatis pedibus,* "feet which have eyes." Brother Thomas reaches a climax of rhetorical obfuscation in this sentence (XII:191–92): *Sed et morientum quidem in morte mortis detruncatio mors est.*

Pronoun references are sometimes left inexplicit or unclear. When we find (XII:17–18) *unae meae atque alterae,* we are evidently meant to supply *litterae,* though the word has not been mentioned. In Brother Thomas's sentence (IX: 114–15) *quid illi abditum natura occuluit, aut quos non lustravit haec auctores?* one can only conclude that *haec* refers to Cereta, though *illi* a few words before has also referred to her. Cereta in v:23 introduces a feminine accusative *(munitam)* which has two possible antecedents, one of them *(unguentum)* in the wrong gender, the other *(arca)* in the wrong case. Brother Thomas also seems sometimes to get his genders confused, as in XII:39–41: *menti tuae . . . quae . . . illustratum, etsi opacum in se sit . . . ,* or in IX:16–18: *rationali . . . appetitu . . . qui . . . in bonum pronus . . . orbatum ipse judicio . . . .* The description of the ass in Cereta's funeral oration alternates constantly between masculine and neuter modifiers, e.g., I:327–28 *at nostrum hoc pistrinense jumentum . . .;* and line 335–36: *quippe qui ausus committere sese. . . .* This ambiguous designaton of gender (which recalls Catullus's references to the emasculated Attis in Poem 63, alternating between masculine and feminine genders) reinforces the mourners' attitude toward the ass as so beloved as to be almost a member of their family.

One of Brother Thomas's most distinctive stylistic quirks is his insertion into his letters of parenthetical apologies *(fateor),* assertions *(inquam),* appeals *(quaeso, obsecro, exoro),* and exclamations *(oi!, dii meliores!, proh dolor!) Inquam,* the most frequent of all his asides, actually has little assertive force; it is introduced at random, once even into a question. It might be added that the apologetic tone implied by *fateor* is sometimes belied by its context, a stinging attack or sarcasm directed at Cereta.

Characteristic of the effusive style of both Cereta and Brother Thomas is a desire for elegant variation, saying the same thing (or nearly so) two, three, or more times in slightly different ways. Thus we get *cecidere, abest, periit, evolavit* IX:155–57); *complana frontem, acumen linguae amputa, obtunde vel calamum* (X:91–92); *aversa . . . facie . . . contracto vultu, labroque presso ac deducto nimbosius cilio* (XI:303–4); *contracto . . . vultu . . . subsannanter . . . provecto . . . labro* (XII:9–11: this and the previous two examples illustrateBrother Thomas's infatuation with circumlocutions relating to anger); *nemo ducem, nemo rectorem expectat* (I:79); *affligor, sollicitor* (I:133); *vendibiliora venalia* (I:141); *raptim cursimque* (I:167–68); *quae curarum intermissiones, quae laxamenta, quod spatium* (I:183–84); *et manes et umbras* (I:196–97); *honorant, venerantur, observant* (V:33–34); *reverentia castitas religio* (VI:15–16); *Despicit numquam. Numquam ad inferiora reflectitur* (XI:182–83). A more subtle device is a grouping of words on a single theme which gradually shifts the meaning to build up to a climax: *superant populantur occidunt* (VI:38); *inquietat inficit exulcerat occidit* (XII:152–53: thus Brother Thomas describes the process by which a tiny gnat can kill a man).

As might be expected in the kind of turgid grand style affected by these authors, elaborate metaphors are introduced which can sometimes get out of hand. Brother Thomas is fond of comparing Cereta to a bee, due to her real or imagined attacks on him (X:1–13; XII:112–14). Cereta calls herself *inter proceras arbores tenue virgultum, ac inter canes Alexandri lepuscula*, "a slender bush among tall trees, and a little rabbit among the hounds of Alexander" (VIII:7–8). Peter's letters are like patched-up furniture which he sets out for sale (IV:3–7). Brother Thomas is a rower in a patched-up dinghy who tries to catch Cereta's fleet of ships, though by the end of the same sentence he has become a woodpecker who is trying to "ape" *(simiare)* her (XII:97–102). Elsewhere in Brother Thomas's menagerie, Cereta becomes a mighty eagle who is wasting her time chasing little birds (XI:38–40).

Brother Thomas also plays on Cereta's name several times. In his strange dream-poem, a voice orders him to "pluck the laurel" (IX:196). The precise point of this is unclear, but it very likely has a sinister connotation, considering the menacing sarcasm which seems to underlie much of Brother Thomas's ostensible praise of her. In X:97, he says that criticism is inappropriate coming from her since "poisons everywhere flee laurel berries."

Among minor eccentricities of grammar we find *ipsus* for *ipse* (I:430), *gratia* preceding rather than following its object (I:80–81), and an active verb used in place of a deponent: *causare* for *causari* (XI:136).

I. DIVAE LAURAE IN ASINARIUM FUNUS ORATIO[1]
(Vt, f. 5r–14r; Ve, f. 11r–24v)

Conglobati gregatim advenae et frequentioris populi lamentabile vulgus, hodie si pastoria lugendi materia ad hos funebres planctus consuluisset musas agrestes, et certum haberet animus, quasnam sedes asinis fata posuerint, vel si doctam me fecisset celebris illa quaestio majorum, quam de animarum circuitione sub obitu iterato Pythagoras Porphyriusque[2] monstrarunt, declamarem miserioris aerumnae contiones et guttatim humectarem vobiscum haec ora lacrimulis. Sed longe certe refert, ut dictura considerem finem orandi, ne aut in complexionis ociore defluxu mergatur epilogus, aut nescia materiae narratio suis se tricis ita perimplicet, ut primos locos post venienda praecurrant. Sciunt enim dicendi magistri consuesse auditorum conceptam spem supra modum offendi, si attentis mentibus insipidior dispositio primum adaurescat[3] et surdior. Hinc solitavit triforas vocum organulas ni respondeant fistulator infringere. Hinc vel ipsa praedita etiam ornatu copiaque dicendi, si ad movendos animos digestione atque arte venerim incondita, majestatis oratoriae mox rea ab munere splendentis eloquentiae proscribar. At cum Theocritus et Stoici atque Peripatetici[4] de animarum immortalitate videantur ambigere, horum auctoritate satis appetitur fides, quod jumenti flatus inanis sit perpetuis umbris addictus. Quare non est Joannes Solde pater orbate abs te uno dirae sortis animalium flenda conditio. Ingemiscamus potius omnes, suspiremus, renovemus animi vulnus. Immo stridulo tuopte susurro praeoccupemus querulum guttur, ac velut dociles imitatores tui conculcata vocum regyrantium murmura volutemus. Erit quippe conveniens hoc satis exordium, quo primum conciliandam emeriti favoris gratiam ad communem hanc tristitudinem mihi nanciscar.

Incipe igitur saucie senex, quem intonsa barba superciliumque gravius ad demonstrationem vitae infelicioris obscurant. Dic, ne te poeniteat, dic lugubre carmen. Respondebimus alterni. Cantabimus armentales heroas dicemusque nemorum deos et ducti circum funeris pangemus maestiter exaequales aerumnas. Surge. Aggrediamur. Tange demonstratam ex sarmento detrito citherulam.* Move plectra ficticia, et volutatas industria tua comesasque voces ab gutture frigutienti resorbe. Sequemur, quoti sedemus. Sequentur et nos primores popularium confertissimi greges. Imitabimur increpentis lyrae qualescumque modos, quos dicacula conquestio tua deplanxerit. His tu elisis praefocatisque garritibus mulcebas memini languentem asellum. Lis ille resonantibus bombis allectus subsequi te solitavit ad stabulum, dum pastus potu pabulatuque rediret. Cognoscet ex his forte numeris dominum suum informe cadaver. Forte exesi jam capitis surdastres auriculae personatos ita clamores accipient. Nonne ex saltantibus ad modulos tibiae lapidibus et Thebas Amphyon[5] et Gnosum Corybantes in Creta[6] fundarunt? Num potuit et harmonicos Orphei concentus Eurydice obita morte sentiscere? Nec multum quidem abest symphonica illa potentia qua ineptientes et dementatos homines Asclepiades sanitati redibuit.[7] Verum in hanc spem haec ita sentiendi Plinius et Seneca me parum adducunt, qui substantias separatas, nedum evanescentes spiritus, in illa tranquilitate reponi voluere post mortem, in qua a sensu ante vitam interquiescebant otiosae. Haec indita est brutis omnibus una mortalitas morte mortalior. Haec impretiabilis perditae vitae jactura. Hoc feralis naturae obligamentum, illud culpatius, cuius vitio, quicquid levatioris animi restabat, jam in maerore poenitissimae consternationis emarcuit. Quare cum persuasibile argumentum nullum mihi supersit ad remedia doloris, non deest luctuosa qu†a†estio cuius amarulentum facinus funestos nimium angores in clamores rurestris huius theatri convertat.

Movendae itaque misericordiae nervis innitemur attentius. Asciscamus desperationi flumen ingenii et medio pelago sollicitatae eloquentiae vela pandamus. Surgite incurvati baculo pastores, vosque delecti agasones, et caprarii melotas vestes sordidati praecedite. Sequantur obsiti squalore muliones, bubulci hos equisonesque sectentur, opilionum dehinc vestigia succedant, mox archimandritae se moveant, illuvies deinde populi certatim ex omni agro densissima gravis circa vecterinum corpus incedat. Ad lacrimas nemo ducem, nemo rectorem expectet. Casum non consilium sequamur. Convenimus ad hoc solenne gratia plangendi. Jam nobis expectatio meliorum nulla superest, quae possit lenire molestias. Jam communis infortunii quo angimur liquet omnibus causa. Caeca sane eorum satis humanitas, qui putant suos planctus in dicentis voce, vultu atque motu pendere. Fons enim pietatis aperitur ex corde, a quo ad oculos via est, unde lacrimarum imber exudat. Conspicite igitur, videte vos ipsi piis oculis humum cruore perfusam, ubi stratas funeque tractas Aselli reliquias laniones (crudele visu) arreptis caesim acutisque cultris excoriant. Ecce grafiunt[8] alii ex urnipedis[9] ungulis ferros. Ecce fraxino pendet bastus,[10] quem circum rigentes paleas discrevere lacera[ta] frusta. En qui distorto capite resupinus atrocioribus dentibus ringitur. En dirae pellis hoc spolium, hasta sublimi gestatum. En stramine agresti extructus est torus, quo super jumentum hoc forma languens igne cremetur. Heri Soldi laborum infelix sociene siccine rasitata cauda aversus traheris ad rogum? Quis siccis oculis hoc sepulchrale specus inspiciat, quod famescentes humi fauces sub obscuro baratro dehiscunt? Quis sine singultu videre queat gracilentum hoc corpus arbuteis jam stramentis obnuptum flammarum globis aduri? Quis tam immemor laudis spargendum hoc cineribus marmor non signet elogio? Quidnam Augusto aut Julio[11] dictatori plus causae fuit quod cariores equos monumento locaverint? Num vincet nos Alexander qui Bucefalo[12] suo grandiore pompa duxit exequias? Non video quid memorandum dederit natura corvo,[13] quem Romana plebs in via Appiae funebrem rogum tradendum jussit exequiis. Idque ob ingenium solum quo haeserat illi humanae vocis expressior imitatrixque loquacitas. Sed heus tu Solde porrecto barbitio villose dic quaes†t†o, dic Asini totiens laudata praeconia. Terge tuos, licet, hos fletus. Sume animi robur. Obstringe maerores, ne mentis tuae serenitas ad omne vel modicum nubilum tua culpa videatur offendi. Permultum certe abest a consilio constanti aetatis infirmitas, et videtur mortalius tibi quam Asino vulnus inflixisse fortuna. Suspendat animum tibi prudentia, et tu teipse doloris hoc dedecus voluntario toleratu declina. Monet hoc ratio, suadet tempus. Jam pyrae fumant incendia. Jam exta spirantia[14] jamque ossa cineria igni medio insinuata concrepitant. Jam ferme deflendum, jam conclamandum est busto. Ah noli amabo tam maestiter vulneribus orbitatis occurrere. Noli imminere totus in lacrimas. En consurrectum est. Omnes arcum substitere gemitibus. Dic aliquid. Strangula imperantes loquellae singultus. Desine conflictari maerore te te. Modulare paululum sub[s]urrantes palato clausulas sub conflexo illo vocum intermissu concisas.

SOLDUS

Proh dolor, o pietas. Non facit ad lacrimas cantus, nec convenit in furenti morbo ridere. Laboriosa quippe nimium animi aegrotantis infirmitas. Non possum, accolae fratres huc populariter admissi, non possum, inquam, inter tot crebros fractosque singultus dare luctui finem. Nec potis est infirmior lapsi animi vis adversus torti cordis motus armari. Affligor, sollicitor aestu curarum; ad mortem adeo frigoribus sunt obsessa praecordia. Neque id sane quidem ab re. Nam fuerat mihi vecterinus* asellus mea vita sat carior. Hunc inter collimitantes finitimos fama erat ex emissario Salvalai atque Asina Arcadiae progenitum. Atqui dum Brixiam Mediolano redirem, steti forte in Cremensium octinundinarum[15] lustralibus campis, ubi frequens undecumque populus, sub receptaculis stationariis, aere proposito vendibiliora venalia vendebat. Hic mihi binoctii somnus in stramentis cum plebe rustica fuit. Verum postridie ubi Asinulum formae perquisitae compositissimum vixque den†ti†tientem adhuc aspexi, denum* lubens in illo auri nummum expendi. Continuo superastitit qui sponsione deposita pro retroagenda mercatura dupplum se argenti repensurum offerret. At neque triplicatum optassem. Adeo tanti mihi fuit emisse. Hunc vero petulcum haud absque sollicito itinere domum egi, velut qui saltatriculus ducebat infrenem se, ultro citroque seorsum. Hic paulatim domi grandescens, quamvis neque calcibus restiterit ulli, neque mordicus tenuerit quempiam, audaculus tamen et minax ita mandebat frena sub dentibus, ut citra me auderet nemo ejus lora manu corripere. Ast ubi surgens aetas mactis artubus adolevit, coepit domo ad pistrillam deferre fruges saxo frangendas, atque inde farinam toleratu dignam deportare prognariter. Vix interim parannuit, quod mutuatos armos usuris diariis collocavit, vecturam onerum ad forum navesque Sabini[16] comportans. Scitis et ipsi vos, quotiens huic ex attigua turri prospiciendo monasterio concessus mendicitatis frumentariae sacculos vicatim ostiatimque detulerit. Quis me centies huius impositum dorso abequitare non vidit? Dii nunc humanorum immemores, quae me posthac vectatio gestabit, aspectu jam decolore senioque cariosum? Ibo num pedes tot vias, an solita mei discursatio ante focum marcebit otiosa? Heu crura in ventum quondam raptim cursimque lata, nunc vero incurvatum bacillo corpus lente regentia. Heu quam me mea tussis screatusque fastidiunt; quam jugi tinnitu aures mihi surdescentius immurmurant. Heu quanto nubilo tenebrantur oculi; quam infirmiter dentetentimque[17] genae masticant. Ecce quomodo resolutum hoc corpus vitalium ardentissimae febres macie palloreque conficiunt. Nunc enim pectoris infecti baratrum putridum introrsus fetorem exhalat. Nunc ingruit extremus vitae abientis anhelitus. Nunc in foveam natura* me relinquent[a] dilabor. Utinam deterius nihil restaret mihi post mortem. In hoc vilior est hominis quam bestiae conditio, quod pejores nos quam intravimus e vita ob noxas eximus. Omnes illae in invicta necessitate mortis injurias fortunae devincunt. Heu propterea quae nam torpenti rugis senectae superrestitit interquiescendi respiratio? Quae curarum intermissiones, quae laxamenta, quod spatium, quae nam erit dehinc alteri vigilantia? Quis elaborabit? Quis solertius incumbet, ne inopi familiae et aegrotanti jam homulo mihi quid desit? O tempus horrendum, o misera mei conditio, o dies, o dolor omni dolore vehementior. Periit ex toto paupertaculae nostrae fidissimum columen. Interii miser. Jam minus est nihilo mihi. Jam video quo traducar, quo me perditum eam infelix. Supervivamne parvulis natis invisus? Aut perspectum ullius spei consilium me ultra tardabit? Quin laqueo exitium mihi defungar? Stat atrox consulti sententia, qua pro consciscenda morte ferro me mea manu transverberem. Sic audacis facti mens pavitans apertum ditis specus adibit. Sic visam tenebrosa in Tartara et manes et umbras. Quis falsum habet, quin primis in faucibus Aselli forte ventum[18] inveniam, qui me senium indol[esc]entem sponte suscipiat?

Laura

Et sortem tuam dolemus omnes et nos tui miseret, Solde grandaeve. Sed nollem te argumentis futilibus argumenta colligere. Nam quamquam tibi desperanti non nihil ignoscam, volenter tamen optarem, ut dares laudi, quod detestatus es tanta abominatione profanius. Certe nescio quis te furor abstulerit, aut qua desperatione proveharis incautus, ut truces has devotiones, haec piamenta gentilium depreceris in mortem, quas grandior aetatis canae barba [prae]respuit,* quasi intestatus fata deum execreris et provoces. Neque enim dolorum est ulla tam imperiosissima vis, quae temperantem virum ab modestia aequilibratae mentis extrudat.* Huius irreverentis culpae vera potius ipse tibi causa es. Orant te astantes catervae circum secus ne devoveas obtundentes hoc genus diritates in deos, quibus profanari consueverunt caelo tacti Gigantes. Jam satis est fletum. Ne torqueat te recordatio praeteriti. Comprime fluctuantes ingeminatasque voces, et quod oportet aegre ne feras. Neque enim sunt flenda mortalia, cum mortuos suspiria nil relevent. Nam quis amissum lugeat frustra? Sed mecum multi sunt in hoc assistentium tanto concursu, qui mortis Aselli causam praescisse desiderent.[19] Tu si plenum acerbitate funus expectas, dic insidiantis fortunae laqueos, quibus hoc toties tanque miseranter vocatum animal perditioni fuit impensum.

Soldus

Arguit me lacera devicti cordis infirmitas, quae tanto in conspectu plebis innumerae sanari non potest. Vulnus enim irremediabilis damni verborum medicina non sustinet. Pudet fateor obligamenti, quo uror impatiens. Sed considerate vos inexorabile fatum, quod me destinat in mortem. Videte me vetulum mei nescium, et barbam pannosamque vestem, sub turpata impoliti[a]e* prolixum. Satis erat superque mihi plangere pectus invisum, absque eo quod intercurreret causa, qua ebullientis miseriae casus sub transverberato corde suspiriosus luctuosusque dictarem. At posteaquam hoc ita fieri necesse est, non sit vobis alienum, qui solliciti funeris congemiscitis mecum, quod heri ad me femina passo capillo per viam advolavit, quae ululatu tristiore nunciaret e profluo monticulo se perditum esse meum Asellum. Procedo fractis lamentis immugiens. Mox in haec verba ruit puer agrarius: Sospes sis (inquit) patercule Solde. Nescio an aspiratione stellarum vel sorte quadam hoc tibi tristius obvenerit, quod flebilis dictu casus Asinum tuum rugatum colla surripuit. Is nanque montivagus dum pabula ex ripis curvatus obiret, illusit illi summota terra pedes incautos, ex quo ab clivosi scopuli jugis in pronae vallis abrupta praecipiti saltu descendit. Ut primum jacuit, mox in occursum lupus incessit, qui seminecis lancinatum discerperet omentum. Ex tunc miser in vultum ruens has coepi ab desperato pectore quaerelas effundere: O Furiae Eumenides, o Cerberi canis, o crinitae Gorgones, o tot hiatus Hydrae saevientis, quae me aperta ardentis Aetnae spiracula volentem excipiant? Aut quid mihi meisque vita nunc prosit? Posteaquam ruit omnis in Asino spes reliqua mea, postquam ruit et omne meorum subsidium? Heu quo nunc fimo pinguescet agellus? Quis ligna gelu, quis messe domum* defalcata farra portabit? Heu cui vivis insane? Ubinam Vulcani latent ignes? Ubi dormiunt fulmina Jovis? Cur non vorago me Charybdis absorbet? Quid non me dehiscentis terrae baratrum ingurgitat?

LAURA

Infelix o tandem atave pronepotum atque tui jam immemor Solde. Quonam te vehis amens? An quo tantus te dolor abducit? Ubi dierum, ubi longae experientiae lucerna? Ubi consultum lumen illud ingenii? Ubi ad rectum vivendi cursum gubernacula tui consilii? Cur ita vellis immites vertice canos? Quis te cogit per devia vitae praecipitare dies? Soli ne tibi sors invida tulit horrendum? Ad crebras variantis Fortunae calamitates gignimur omnes. Si miserior te planctus, si acerbitatum vincit aculeus, liceat potius tui causa lugere, qui rationale et deo dignum animal ex hac mortalitate effugis via praecipiti. Porro si bruti moveret ulla te pietas, consolari deberes quod prop terea longior ipsius peregrinatio jam finiit, ut esset quo tandem aetas discruciata quiesceret. Pangit non flet genitor, si quando sospes natus ad portum post naufragium enavit. Ita vegetissimum hoc quondam animal tuum, multis ac variis laborum turbinibus actum* et longos fati[g]ationum fluctus expertum,* exivit tandem plenam mali diem, quam in protractu aevi tardioris non potuisset effugere. Est enim vitae spatium, qualecunque sit illud, una mortis eademque vigilia. Nec obitu quid opportunius animantibus natura providit. Doleo magis quod fluctuans et fracta jam haec aetas tua sit laesa tot annis. Efflanda unicuique tandem anima est. Sed tuam senectutem nimium vicina mors insequitur.* Adeo improvisus omnibus properantis vitae finis accelerat. Absint igitur istae querelae ab tuis labiis atque oculis procul, ne in desperatione dicaris morti ante tempus ostia repandere. Senescat ergo corpus, non senescat animus immortalitate donatus. Quin age potius recordare tui, ne sperne vota faventium. Flecte rogo retroque verte consilium, et attende animo quid tua declamet oratrix. Quod si non flecteris nostris oratibus, vincant te perculsi tuis luctibus liberi. Moveat uxor, quam tuus maeror tenet in lacrimis. Tangat saltem syncopis* filiae tuae ex colapsu mortuae potius quam dormienti similimae, in quam crines vestesque solutam mortalis acerbitatum dolor incruduit. Satis hucusque causas lacrimarum ediximus. Satis optarem nunc suffectum mihi dari, qui pensitatius Aselli vitam moresque cognoverit. Conticescant igitur omnes quaqueversum attentiore silentio. O[ret]* unus rerum instructior, ut et persuasionis plenior formetur inventio, et redeat dic[u]ndum* funus, unde defluxit. Nec mora, insurgunt dicturi mille certatim.* Sed audaculus quidam e pueritio Philonacus tali ex nimbo popularitatis in orchestram voce descendit.

Philonacus

Miramini promptum video Patres arvorum, quod dux ovium horridulus, et genas adhuc depilis cretatusque pedes atque scalatim[20] decalvatus caput (ut cernitis) hoc caespitium tribunal tam insolenti supercilio dicturus intraverim. Sed oro, ne credite quod huc venerim quia bellus mihi videar aut supra nostrates regulos me decaregem existimem. Veni potius ut hoc me meamque culpam causatius[21] expurget. Quoniam praesto sum, quocunque de Asello vectore inquisitio se verterit. Velut qui suppeditatos labores ejus usu experientiaque didicerim. Ego nanque e Soldi famulitio vernale mancipium obsequiis dudum occurro servilibus. Nec recensuerim qui pater meus, postquam a stipendiis abiit emeritus. Huius gradarii fratrem pullulum* adhuc velut abigeus* abduxerit. Hunc narrabat fratrem pullulum coquinatum matri dedisse, ut elixis cum capite et pulmone visceribus quod reliquum esset ligneis inassaretur verubus, ad quo tandem exhalaret nidor, certus ille fumantis cocturae praenuntius. His epulis voluit duobus lurconibus sociis parari convivium, qui cana gula ad primam mensam esui dedere penitus totas* jus omne non calice sed concha sorbentes, velut qui gloriarentur majore sapore, aliud nunquam animal ligurisse, tanta illius condimenti fuerat industria. At nostrum hoc pistrinense jumentum in sudore operosisque negotiis eximium, fortius* semper in ipsa onerum continuatione surgebat, praebebatque saepiculae raedis colla pertrita, ad quae pro meritorio curru trahendo miros conatus exhibuit. Et quamquam varios primum rotarum strepitus[22] et pavorem ex micantibus auriculis arrectisque jubis atque superbis naribus salt†u†ando spirarit, didicit tamen cervicem arduam capistro obedienti submittere et securiores vias ab frementis urbis incursu vel minaci transire. Quippe qui ausus committere se se fluminibus unda a* transitu nunquam intremuit. Neque ulla fontium ad bibendum fuit illi discretio. Potum sponte bibax non sibilo quopiam allectus hausit innixius.[23] Is quotiens a cratium praesepibus solutus exiliit, occursavit hero tellurem gestibundus excavans. Quadrupedavit autem cominus volutatu pulverans se se, remeavitque domum falcata cauda, atque explicatissimis gressibus liber. Nunquam enim cogendus verberibus erat in cursum, si quo forte quam mox properandum aut citatius inde remigrandum fuit. Nam praeter ceterorum sui generis inertiam ocissimus pernicissimusque currebat. Testis est Brixia, ubi ludis Augustis insistente me et sollicito omnium intuitu primus ad metam currendi palmam obtinuit. Huc ille aspectu torvus isurgens stare loco nesciebat. Sed impatienti* victoria, triumphatuque superbiens, in obvios quoscunque,* vel barbaros equos procax contentiosusque resistit. Quid mitius, quid submissius isto gradario, qui versicolore tapete coopertus sororem meam turrito vertice et sertis involutisque textu crispato crinibus ornatam molliter sub alterno illo crurium explicatu vexit ad nuptias? Fecit et valentioris firmitatis suae periculum, quod supra omnium onus mecum etiam nunc multi decantant, quando rediens Breno Pisognas toto illo atque curvo viarum anfractu sustulit ferri libras pondo quingentas. Videbor attingere quae supra fidem sunt, si dixero pluviarum agnitionem indocili animalis huius imperitiae connexam. Cuius auriculae pulsi†ta†tae frequentius* decretorios adeo praemonebant imbres, ut nunquam me fefellerint denuntiata pronostica. Parum est quod ferrandos ultro pedes fabro commiserit? Adde quod meridiantes sopitis cunis infantes mulcenti ex arteriis in auras voce fovebat. Nos vero pubertate minores expergisci consuevit anteluculo, suis illis rugitibus rasas asperius voces implentibus. Modum autem admirationis egreditur, quod somni parcissimus a cadente vespera ad surgentem auroram totiens infesto rictu detonuit, quot coeptabant horae sentisci. Erat hoc unum fessi pueritii gestamen, quod nos quosque ab arvis redeuntes ex refusis limo scrobibus abduxit tris saepe ex nobis dorso recipiens neque ad primas usque tenebras quemquam omnino succusans (ni forte quispiam equitandi nescius prae timore ceciderit). Erat enim versi dexter ad manum utrobique declinans. Nec omiserim quod detegendae culpae meae patrocinari didicit mali nescius, ubi nocte fruges furtim ex acutaque falce subtraherem. Sane fuit et ita moriger ut ex ulla renitenti contumacia neque aculeos unquam neque flabra pertulerit.* Fatebor tamen impietatis meae piaculum, culpatione cuius angor infestius quotiens reminiscor, quod iratus carnifex hunc ego fustibus caesum verberando multavi, quando se pro scabiei sordibus diluendis in flumine mergi noluerit. Ex hoc ille stupentibus in terram oculis dolorem ostendens et continuo trinoctio se se a cibatu continuit et in pedes se nunquam recepit interdiu. At vero postridie cum plusculi de plebe eo, ubi pascebatur, recepissemus in pratis, ut illius equitatu mutuo de more lusitaremus cursaremusque, hunc ut primum alter mecum inscendit, mox vindex calcitro retroversus instans lubrica via recessit nec desiit infestis pedibus verberatas auras abrumpere, usque dum nos atque alios imberbes quotquot insedebant a tergore atque armo passim excuteret. Risimus omnes opportuno joco faceti, et fecit unum varia indignatio ridiculum. Sed casus ille acerbius multo mihi animum momordit, qui percussum gen dolebam. Nec tum adeo movit ille risum pueris late depulsis, quantum movere ipse lacrimas illi parabam. Ita sub ardenti ultionis cura conticescens expectavi serotinum vesper,* sub quo reum injuriae medio in arboreto pressius deligatum feris exposui. Sane hiemabat umbrosum loci nemus ursa ferociens e cuius uberibus gemina lambens fetura pendebat. Haec noctivaga dum cibum praeceps odore vestigat inventae superingruit bestiae, quae ubi impendens necessitas incubuit, impetum ferae spumantis hostilemque famem ictibus atque morsu procul abegit. Ast ego somnii monitu imaginatus hoc proelium, ut exivi a quiete perterritus mox a nocte multa surrexi, et nunc domo huc nunc illuc abiens ac rediens. Intuebar astra caeli cadentis, quae rubescentes matutini radios expectato sub oriente nuntiarent. Sol nondum adhuc sub nostro polo coeperat oriri. Quod impexus vixque districtus perpropere silvae silentia praecucurri, ut inspectandam aeripedis sortem agnoscerem. Prospicio. Hunc vinctum adhuc praeter opinionem intueor. Accedo propius. Erat jam meatus animae gravior, in ultimo prope expirantis hiatu, velut qui transversa obtortis intueretur luminibus, et spiritum intra illa obstructum vix anhelis naribus efflaret. Adeo seminecis vires atque animum expectoraverant timor et labor. Hunc ego subitariis manibus solutum cogo ab opacis ad solem. Jam crura ipsius itioni frigida obstupuerant horrore formidinis. Sic operosum mihi fuit hunc exanimatum adhuc domum hinc ferula minaci propellere. Hac ipse pigriore tarditate iam fessus fastiditusque anteibam comminus, ceu qui altius mecum animo cogitarem, qua me possem de Aselli conflictu excusatione tueri. Is vero ipsus primi sub lapidis ab urbe diverticulo hinc ad laevam in torcular angiporti concessit, ubi ventrem siti correptum, uvis mustoque replevit. Hoc vinatico potu atque ejus adorato vapore suffusus, coepit fanatico primum furore discurrere. Plenisomno dehinc sopore domi biduum jacuit. Haec una suspicio consideratum erum invasit, quod invidia malorum hippomanes forte sucum maleficae medicatum obdormienti bestiae substraverit. Vel boletum potius ipsa vipereum, luridive aconiti frondes noxio pastu decerpserit. Hinc accersitus medicus aegrum hoc animal consulto ferri candentis antidoto a sopitis sensibus ad pervigilium derepente restituit. Interea vinitores apparent, qui pro reficiendis uvis diem domino dicant ad curiam. Ibi actionem e diverso coram judice vicissitudo partium cavillationum mutuo colludio propugnat. Stat demum praetoris arbitratu adversus Soldum, opportuni damni mulctatitia pecunia. Is vadari jussus. Tritam pignori melotem atque nodosum baculum syringanque deposuit. Verum hanc temulentam animadversionis usuram impastus Asellus menstruo jejunio dissolvit, dum subnascentes carduos foliaque decidua jam et dumeta spinea dentitio stupenti totumdit. Sic evenit miseris, ut fidem frontemque tandem amittant longi servitii. Hoc igitur est unum illud scelus infandum, haec irrita audacia, haec torva atque inulta illa crudelitas, qua despicabilis mali auctor, tam inclementer, tam cruente, tam barbare degrassatus sum adversus insontem. O sceleratum me, non undis solum Tantali, sed Cocytiae paludi ad os usque mergendum. Heu quae me posthac hospita tellus, quae me miserum domus excipiet? Heu quisnam me leo Nemaeus, quis Erymanthus aper, quae tigris Hyrcana[24] diris illis unguibus dentatoque rictu laniandum ipso jure devoret? Proripiendus sum fateor, nudandus caedendusque flagro, quod scelere furoris accensus suppliciis innocentem affeci. Fuitne Solde refugium hoc tuum a nobis defamulatione* latrunculis tam improbe, tam acerbe diriterve cruciandum? Num debuit firmior paupertinae vitae tuae basis ab resecandis manibus meis ita tractari? Quid mirum arbitramini vos e tot milibus viri gregales, si vetulum hunc pridem pro animo fracto repraehensum ad dementem forte lamentationem devius damni dolor abduxit? Miretur potius qui non meminerit quantae acerbitatis sit nequicquam optatiora planxisse.

Dic tu Laura Demosthenis majestate praeclara. Quis patrem familias egenum, quis senem aegrotum in morte gestatoris sui flere prohibeat? Mors enim ac paupertas et servitus in animo vel constanti ignitas saepe dolorum faces accendunt. Parce igitur ipsa potius afflicto illacrimare mecum. Dic ea stilo misericordiore praeconia quae rationibus ornate distinctis mortale hoc insidiantis paenitentiae vulnus obverberet. Habe jam vicariam hanc orandi cathedram, in qua ex tempore praecarioque suffectus, tametsi nullis sim litterulis imbutus et nulla auctoritate nullove aspectu aut specie nitoris adductus, projectos tamen quoquomodo potui et nugis nugatiores fluctus effudi. Tu vero eloquio nata puella, quae in hoc isto campo pro deflendis comitiis proque funebri senatu vocata declamitas, revoca nunc, oro, memoriae tuae felicitatem par regno satis habendam. Sparge nunc ore virgineo Quintiliani nectaris latices instar puri fontis caste pudiceque manantes. Quibus pro movendae pietatis exigentia quod reliquum superest orationis amicias. Expectant ovium boumque magistri dulciloquae tuae buccae splendores, qui arescentes omnium oculos in demulcenda jamtandem animorum tranquillitate concilient.

Laura

Audistis turbae rurestres vosque pelliti monticolae quid tumidus iste gulam agrarius super his quae funeris sunt suspiriosa narratione percensuit. Enitar ipsa nunc pro causae nervis ea complecti quae possint figuris suis et suasibili argumento vestros animos ad arbitrium a dolore subvehere. Fiet autem elaborate (quantum in me est) non quod huic me pignori tantum obstringam,* ut si non persuasero velim oratricis nomen amittere. Nam Aesculapius et Cicero quamvis medelis alter, alter omnibus eloquentia praestiterit, non sanavit ille tamen omnes Hippolytos neque hic semper pro Milone[25] suasit. Nec tacebo quod puer iste vulpecula primo vix lanuginis flore vestitus hoc adinvenerit aucupium, ab mea dicendi jejunitate prorsus abhorrens, quo agreste meum ingenium et stilum ipsum femineo sexu languentem atque gestus omnis incultos sub viscario laudis fraudatae tentavit. Et quanquam in illo rusticitatis genere trito multa probe solo ipso habitu atque gratia naturae sine arte distinxerit, urget me tamen atque mordet maesta illa tyrannidis atrocioris injuria qua eversor humanitatis. Iste rusticulus, non legis modo Porciae aut censurae Semproniae, sed tribunitii[26] carceris secures emeruit, quippe qui pro ingenii portiuncula apte satis atque facete cuncta digesserat, si inter recensendum* historiam illata illa verbera atque excandescentes injurias inconsideratus asinicida transisset. Atqui hac una contumelia servili paterculus noster exardens acerbius praeter quam alias unquam indoluit, cum renovari sensit comploratam miserationis imaginem, quae e pacatis nunc quasi praecordiis exciderat. Consideremus ipsi nos, quae parata indignatio cordis occurreret quaeve suffusa menti amaritudo ferbesceret,* si sentiremus cum pulsatione convitioque violatum, qui continuis laboribus suis suppetias rebus nostris, praesidia accessionesque portaret. Certe si mores atque vitam recapitulemus veredi nostratis, non fuit unquam quo debuerit in ipsum perperam aliquid injuria popularis incessere. Fuit potius praeferendum onagris animal, et calcaribus stragulis epiphiis, freno, sella dignissimum. At nunc posteaquam annosam illius strangulavit ultima hora vitam, referendum est exquisitis odoribus corpus, immo vel Cypricis unguentis et nardo liniendum. Nec dixisse rubor erit, quod sit pompa rituque regum deferendum exequiis et sua pro rostris oratione donandum. Nolo mirum videri si e geminis Asellis alterum comedones illi mandiderint, alterum fuerit a Soldo aere tanto mercatus, cum et burdones hoc genus epulandos instituerit Maecenas antiquis et unum Q. Asius nummis comperaverit quadringentis. Hoc unum est ex omni genere animantium, quod prae ceteris Sylvanus pecoris deus numine suo tutatur. Hoc isto ad matris deum solenne Silenus vectus est. Huius maxime Priapus immolatione laetatur. Huius lineamentis Apuleius[27] circumvestiri se voluit. Huic Romae similem Cornelius Asina[28] cum dotis onere pro sponsorio pignore filiae produxit in forum. Huius pelle tensius in tympanum tracta iens in proelia Mavors[29] utitur, atque sono clangenti surgentes e diversoque sibi concurrentes hostes redivivis cruentantur ultro vulneribus. His visus est Plato[30] sensisse congruentius inversari animas eorum, qui turpitudinis incentivo servientes voluptuarie ex hac vita decesserunt. Quid ultra? Asellos prioris aevi religio sub duabus autumnalibus stellulis, in capite cancri fulgentibus et digito in caelum et sua nomenclatura monstravit, quasi senserit illos e tantis vitae poenis ad curam humani laboris habendam in caelum esse translatos. Asinis Romae consules ludos caelebrarunt in circo, ob id quod essent vehiculo solis generatoris adacti. Magna tibi dolorum esse debet refrigeratrix haec ratio, immo certa ad aeternam memoriam via, quod possederis tale jumentum, cui rudes atque sine litteris gentes multae sacrificent. Sed haec fidei sunt. Tangamus lucrosissimas partes, quas vigilius medendi studium invenit. Asinini gregis comitatu non erubuit inter uxores Neronis Poppaea[31] procedere. Tanta politiei* atque oris tenerescentiae* ex balneo lactis huius custoditur utilitas. Atqui natura nihil relinquens occultum, hoc isto lacte Chirogricis[32] atque percussis infantumque febribus ac dolentibus puerperae mammis efficacius nihil medicatiusve censetur. Fertur et eorum sanguis ephemeri prodesse et quartanariis morboque regio. Conferunt pthisicis[33] atque iliacis carnes elixae, sed verrucis ac renibus urina non mediocre remedium. Fimus vero et pilorum cineres pituitae non minus quam sanguinis profluvio crispandisque comis auxiliantur. Prosunt et sequacibus quae serpunt ulcusculis ungulae pulveratae subtilius quarum maxime suffitu ita pili nascituri succrescunt, sicut utero obedit evocatus abortus. Magna est ostentatio medicamenti in jecore adversus epileuthicos* comitialesque pueros, quibus etiam a nocturno lemurum pavore sanandis substrata pellis indulget. Sunt qui scripserint deciduos spissari capillos, si ter a genitalium intersperso pulvere liniantur. Pulchrescit mire cicatrix ex adipe atque illo adusta vel tosta solibus pellis; et nodosi emendantur, ac scrophulae. At vermes pulmonis enecat fumus. Ex his in magicis multa traduntur in quibus certi nihil sub nimia illa subtilitate dinoscitur. Levavit et asinos ab hac hominum pilosorumque animalium utilitate natura, ut pediculos nesciant, quorum injuria vates Alcmaeon[34] dictatorque Sulla[35] et rector Judeae Pilatus fastidiendi perierunt.

Ad tollendos nunc omnis animi scrupulos peraeque et praemonet, quod is ipsus Asellus antecellens alios plurima certe fecit, quae ad memoriam in posteros transmissa docti cantabunt. Hinc erit Solde pater tuo nomini gratum, quod illius gesta praeclara aeternis litteris scriptores multi mandaverint. Quare quamquam inter Syrtes* ac Scyllam mediis inhorrescentium malorum turbinibus agaris, deberent tamen huius te sepulti merita solari, quod datum sit tibi tot annis illo fruisci. Considera aequiore animo quanto usui tibi fuerit quantaque usura reddiderit quod accepit. Cogita quam bone frugi assecla se tibi exhibuerit semper. Attende quotnam virtute sua aborigenum copias in his campis desolatoriis attraxerit. Pensa quaeso qua gratia, qua benivolentia, quibus studiis haec concomitantium tanta caterva te complectitur, consolatur, hortatur. Testis est flebilis illa vox omnium, quae aegritudinem animi tui miserata tot lacrimis tantoque gemitu desaevit[36] in auras. Plangantur hi, quibus satis mori non fuit, ni vel piscibus naufragi vel inhumati volucribus aut putrescentes vermibus sepeliendos se vorandosque crediderint. Iis hoc ustum jam atque collectum cadaver caret injuriis. Ecce locatos cineres recens urna contexit. Ecce visendis tumuli saxis insculptum illius nomen affigitur. Ecce ad posteros ex annosa quaercu annosiora spolia pendebunt. Ecce vel arbores ipsae agere tibi laudes gestiunt. Ecce qui tristius circum astant greges armenti, quasi ad affligentem te te haec[37] omnes immugiant. Quid Solde te perdis? Quid ineluctabilis Fortunae suggeris causas? Quid isthaec in cassum tristia revolvis? Quid actae jam huic tristitudini tantum indulges? Quid repetis obitus beatissimi memorabilem casum, cuius morte immortalis efficeris? Num forte nescis Fortunam maeroribus saepe gravidam peperisse laetitiam? Una est ab Deis atque morte nostra felicitas. Invitant haec omnia te nimis anxium ad tenenda totius quaerimoniae silentia. Hodie si forti pectore contrarios tuleris casus, si te in adversis fortuna non fregerit, si in sollicitos curarum ardores animus involaverit armatus, quantas quam celebres, quam multas laudes comparabis praedicato illi nomini tuo. Quod vel adusque magnum illud orbis incendium nulla nesciet omnino posteritas?[38] Insinuamus nunc merita funeri longo praetexta. Fortunam ex perdito asello injuriae convitiis accusas; quam satius laudare pro gloriae immor-talitate debueras. Sed esto. Nunc saltem eam tu vince ratione, quae te sensu vicit humanitas. Ecce jam persuasi omnes, se sibi restituunt. Sola ego tecum consolanda nunc videor, quae consolatura deveni. Oro te: habe monita nostra non parvi. Habe maximi tot vota plangentium. Cura amicorum tenere sententiam. Oboedi legibus naturae, quae te primum tibi commendant, ne velis ob amorem possessi mancipii ab cassa vita te per†it†are seminecem. Est enim ab re eorum dolere, quibus reminiscaris in cassum. Non angat igitur atrox illa te peroratio rusticuli. Consule animae, quam vel in primis labiis trahis exiguam. Ecce satis a nobis tecum est itum ad lacrimas. Jam satis unguibus ora turpavimus. Jam superexercitati spiritus ab hac illa tui turbulentia subducendi sunt, cuius recordationis impulsu hanc atram diem tam maeste miseranterque defle[vi]sti. Ne ejula. Ne plange super eo pater annose, qui nullus est. Non curant (crede fideli) nostros gemitus inferi, et voces nostras defuncti non audiunt. Fabulosum est quod errent animae relictis corporibus vagae. Frustra jam pridem ipse tu aselli nomen ad auriculam inclamasti vehementius. Praeteritum sola vincit oblivio, et lenit ratio sola maerores. Parce igitur luctui. Comprime fletum. Restringe singultus immites. Jam consolatior si velis tibi restat copia vivendi. Jam coepit dies sub primis tenebris caligata noctescere. Jam audientium ora languida inquietos funeri clamores immiscent. Satis jam praeficae hac funeris impolitie foedatae discerpuere crines. Sat filii atque nurus in particulas jam diloricavere semilaceras vestes. Ecce in quotovis agmine populi jam aestuans fervor omnis tuae acerbitatis incanduit. Eamus. Exue quicquid nigricat circum. Surge jam tandem. Hora nos admonet. Ecce passim jam undique surgunt instrepentia crispantium* convenarum examina. Duc ea domum. Sequentur te quacunque iter est. Sume lyram. Dic popinalis fabulae pultarium. Imitabitur te quantislibet modis discipula responsio. Incipe. Revoca ruminante palato garulos alternantesque cantus. Neque intercisas formiculatim voces sub vario derosoque plausu te concinuisse poeniteat. Jam in trajectu orationis Salve atque Vale omnia resonuere.

II. Laura Cerete Benedicto Arsago Papiensi. S.[1]

(Vt, f. 14v–15r; Ve, f. 28r–28v)

Ingenii nostri primitiis donare consuevimus eos, qui peregrina stirpe oriundi ad patriam veniunt. Neque id certe, ut aliquid de nobis jactantius aut populo teste profiteamur. Male enim se temperat qui contra praecepta Socratis se profitetur esse sapientem. Nos de industria potius id facimus, ut et exteri fruantur nostris officiis, et studium nostrum immortalitati fiat acceptius. Neque enim video quomodo scientia ulli rei esse possit, si occultetur absconsa; nam quod premium, qui fructus esse litteris potest, nisi cum fenore celebritatis proferantur* in medium? Ego igitur mihi intra focos patrios deosque penates nihil esse proprium duco, nisi quod nostrum nomen aeternitati commendet. Vale. xiii Kal. Aug.

III. Benedicto Arsago Papiensi Laura Cereta. S.[1]

(Vt, f.15r; Ve, f. 28v–29r)

Qui te erudiat Apollo, et quos fontes colas, quaeve te lactent Musae, ex litteris tuis satis assequor, sive has illas tibi Pierides sive Castalides[2] forte dictaverint. Misisti enim ad nos limatiorem epistolam tuam, quam velut instar coronae ex utriusque linguae rosulis[3] atque foliis lauri intercursantibus textam cum vimine eloquentiae ligasti. Omnes enim Heliconis circum ripae muscosae, omnia vel Parnassi prata pulchrescentes jam tibi flores ostendunt. Sic studio Nympharum iter ingressus equo curris Bellorophontis[4] ad famam. Vale. viiii Kal. Aug.

IV. LAURA CERETE PETRO SERINAE VIRO. S.[1]

(Vt, f. 16v; Ve, f. 32r–33r)

Ex litteris tuis et rivi alti flagrantis incendia et rerum tuarum summam camino inundanti prope conjectam non absque paventis animi horrore conspeximus. Quare optatius nobis nihil est, quam ut pannosae supellectilis tuae reliquias prae ceteris venaliciis mercatoribus ita divendites, ut sine* proxeneta is te emptor exquirat, qui contra merces commodum argentum opponat. Quod autem scribis te a me minus amari, nescio an serio instes an te ludere mecum existimem. Perturbas me tamen ab re et fidei uxoriae integerrimum cultum subdola loci adulatione metiris. Sed, mi vir, amabo, quid tibi est quod his assentatiunculis me tibi demulces? An forte credam expectes arte me comaturam comas ad tuum adventum, aut sub expolita facie me simulaturam tibi blanditias? Aucupentur potius gratiam conjugum intestatae mulieres, quae ludibundis oculis sollicitae propriae virtuti non fidunt. Est enim istaec vulpinaris adulatio captiosi aucupii viscarium.* Hoc ego te nolim a me tanti mercari. Neque enim ea sum quae plus verborum habeam quam officii. Sum verius tua illa Laura, cui tecum est eadem anima vicissim optata. Vale. Idibus Augusti.[2]

v. Ad Reverendissimum Episcopum Brixie D.D. Paulum Zane super incustodita Eucharistia Laura Cerete Conquestio[1]

(Vt, f. 4r–5r; Ve, f. 25r–27r)

Catholica ecclesiae Romanae respublica* rogatam decreti[2] formulam tenet, quam de reliquiis et veneratione sanctorum celebris consistorii sanctio percensuit. Hoc institutum a patribus nostris quanta observatione sit cautum, satis ex custoditis mandatorum tabulis atque arca testamenti, et figura Mosaici serpentis[3] elicitur. Romae vero apud basilicarum diversos aditus diversae ostenduntur imagines, quas peregre profecti multo cum honore suscipiunt.* Testis est Christi lineamentum illud umbratile, quod in sacrario prominenti reconditum ex Veronicae[4] sudario monstratur. Testis vel frequentata illa virginis matris effigies, ad quam in sancta sanctorum visendam non intrat femina limen. Nec mirum si nostri sub honorariis tabulis provehunt indigetes, morte non minus quam vita probatos, cum gentilium errores impii* Apollinis simulacrum apud Athenas in locu†tu†li aere coluerint. Idolum quoque Jovis Tonantis, et reliquias Danaum,[5] atque Deum matrem, Sibyllinos quoque libros Romani patres in summo Capitolio summa religione servarunt. Hic perpetuis excubiis insomnes illae virgines vivam flammam in Vestae delubro sollicitant.[6] Alexander autem Macedo Darii odoratius unguentum arca tenebat, auro atque gemmis non minus quam custodela munitam. Cantitant multi poetae aureum vellus in Colchide,[7] et Hesperidum poma ex auro micantia a squameo apud Atlantidas[8] dracone tueri. Est et fama recens mille passibus prope Maometi sepulchrum venerabundos Saracenos non assistere. Romano item imperio potitus Alexander Virgilii et Ciceronis imagines in ara custodiri mandavit.[9] Scimus et Hispanos imperatorium Julii Caesaris caput ex sculptili marmore prope Gades[10] inter donaria religiose sacrasse. At fideliores Christiani crucis Domini lignum atque spinas et clavos in sacretioribus* larariis honorant, venerantur, observant. Jam vero apostolorum atque martyrum ossibus innocentiumque corpusculis omnes undecunque illustrantur ecclesiae. Solus omnipotens* Deus, ille tantae majestatis, hominum rex a sacerdotibus legis non tantidem aestimatur, quanti non dixerim paganorum irrita figmenta,[11] sed ne vel mortua ipsa possessio auri atque argenti, quae sub flatura signatae pecuniae repositioni mandatur. Exemplo satis est pretiosissimus Venetorum ille thesaurus, quem novit tua claritas quibus consueverit custodibus, quotove muri ambitu et quantis ferramentis, quot vectibus, quamque quoque forti ostio tutari. Sed ea sinamus quae habentur pretii permulti. Quis rebus suis tam iratus, quis tam prodigus aeris, qui propalam in medio talenta vel margaritum vestesque relinquat? En semirutum nostrum hoc templum quomodo sub laceris culminibus languet. Inclamatum custodem evocare non est opus. Nullus* novit iste locus excubias. Jam reclusos fores nemo depalmat. Omnibus nanque liber aeque patet ingressus atque regressus.* Hostia nullum omnino pessulum, nullus obex, nulla unquam sera perstringit. Clamabant hodie ex illo obsito* loculo prolatae reliquiae. Ignoscimus vobis ingrati fideles, non ignoscit Deus, quod tam vilis hospitii immeritissima sede suscipiatis coaeternum patri genitum, cuius humanitatis carnem atque sanguinem furatrinus*[12] quisque sacrilegus surripere potest, vendere, violare, calcare. Sic ergo filii Dei supradivinissimum corpus in manu relinquitur gentium.[13] Sic magi et sagae noctivagae parata nunc habent altaria, super quibus inferialia mortuis piamenta sacrificent. Haec quanquam non sint professionis indoctae mulierculae, quae satis acquiescit his quae Pontificum decreta sanxerunt,[14] huic tamen opinioni mens non accedit, quod Judeae virginis unigenitus immensus rursus debeat sub aperto delubro et nocte et interdiu in impiorum soluta libertate relinqui. Quod si haec audacula forte quaestiuncula a tramite veritatis aberrat, ego te consumatissimum praesulem, integerrimum, omnisque leges eruditum obtestor, ut hac in re quid tenendum sit quidve dediscendum me tibi in Christo filiolam instituas. Undecimo Chal. Octobres.[15]

vi. Laura Cerete ad Helenam Caesaream de adventu Turchorum. Epistola[1]

(Vt, f. 15v–16v; Ve, f. 30r–32r)

Audisti? Jam fama crevit, et fatetur unum os omnium quod privatus pridem insusurraverat rumor. Non est quod multi praedicant non omnino credendum. Predatoria Ottomani classis trajecit Appuliam.[2] Hui, peramarum nimis est, quod hominis vitam post omnia pessundat. Quis tam excors, ut ingruentia sortis vicinae fata non metuat? Superstitibus nobis exemplo est tyranni in majores nostros truculenta crudelitas. Nonne et nunc audire tibi videtur* Constantinopolitanae cladis[3] Chalcidiique[4] ruinae et Scutrii*[5] clamores illos caelum quondam in stuporem terramque miscentes? Ibi (si recolis) trucidati sunt bello fortissimi duces, obtruncati reges, eversa regna, captivi superbia iraque caesi, inhumata vero cadavera in mare projecta. Nulla barbaro in superatos humanitas, nulla in matronas vel sacratas et virgines reverentia, nulla castitas, nulla religio. Secta caesim Christianorum capita voluptatis suae spectaculum fecit. Omnia vindex in bustum Iliadis, omnia in Pergama incensa convertit, omnia victor superbo fastu perlustrat. Haec (si sapimus) de nobis exempli loco patrata, immo parata pensabimus. Is enim animositatis paternae sectator immo inflammatus certe transgressor, nos invisos fidei suae Christianos ultrici et sanguine stillanti machaera notavit. Sic via discipula, quos inquietavit populos pater, rursus assurgens heres insequitur. Quod si descenderint in Italiam arcitenentium nubes illae Turchorum, quaenam putas erit nobis defensionis certa securitas? Quid facient populorum miserae gentes, si venerit Thrax leo[6] ille bellipotens? Num aliae ad alias imbelles forte recurrent? Jam elanguerunt animi, jam caritatis amor emarcuit. Nulla restitit nobis circumcursatio latibuli, nullum ad tutelares amicos omnino refugium. Possunt transacta futuris magna in parte conferri. Omnes alterutrius calamitatibus ignoscimus, solamur oppressos, miseremur excidii. Nec est invenire tamen, qui contra porrigat ulla subsidia. Adeo spe fallimur omnes, obcaecamur odio, avaritia tenemur. Christianam rempublicam nemo tuetur, in commune nemo consultat. Interim magis invalescunt hostes, qui arte nos provocant in bellum, superant, populantur, occidunt. Cogita, soror, morte nobis unam fore quietem, neque aliam quam sepulchrum victis domum expecta. Non sum Cassandra tamen, quae excidium Trojae casurae longo ante planctu praenuntiem. Sum potius puella simplicior, quam vel occipitio sola documenta fidelitatis inoculant. Ex praeteritorum enim speculo post venientia cernuntur. Unus semper caeli conditor manet, una lex, unus ordo naturae. Soli nos ab deo nitimur aversi. Facti sumus exleges, et a feris mentibus omne jugum humanitatis excussimus. Ex alto autem ignoscentiae nostrae sunt. Cognoscamus, emendemus nostros errores. Cervices paremus obedientiae, non cultro. Ingemiscamus, praesentemus nostras lacrimas Deo. Iram nanque dei lacrimis perituri Ninivitae[7] laverunt. Nam ille clementissimus hominum Pater, velut Israelitici populi sui misertus, superbissimi exercitus Pharaonis,[8] tot volutatas galeas, tot abrepta scuta totque corpora rubro mari correpta subvertit. Novit enim ille (si peccati poeniteat) ex postliminio nos exules pio sinu suscipere. Renunciemus igitur inanibus desideriis, abnegemus saeculi pompas.[9] Cognoscamus opportuni dominum nostrum, qui totiens fideliores sibi servos de pelagi profundo deque mediis incendiis atque ipsis dirae mortis faucibus abductos misericordia sua salvavit. Vale. xiii Chal. Januarias.

VII. LAURA CERETE FELICI TADINO PHYSICO S.[1]
(Vt, f. 14v; Ve, f. 27r–28r)

Naufragantis universi diluvium postquam Deucalionem ac Pyrrham undivaga rate salvavit, mox satores illi hominum sparsis in semine petris obeuntia circum arva replerunt. Hinc altera nasci, hinc reparari coepta est humana respublica cuius lapidescentes adhuc primitiae Martinengi ex integro scilice* moenia fundarunt. Ibi postero* tibi avos atque atavos ex scabris credo cotibus natos natura concessit, a quibus non degeneras quercu ferroque rigidior.* Haec ego non chiromantice[2] aut infando vaticinio perquisii. Liquent mihi perspicue potius ex illa adamantina silentii obstinatione, qua tam duriter abuteris in talem amicum, amicis omnibus desiderio tibi fidissimum. Sane is cognatione mihi pariter et filiolo tuo spiritu pater est cuius amicitiae fores tibi sunt ad omne imperium non minus quam gratiam semper apertae. Is inquam Silvester ille tuus est, a te dudum relegatus,[3] qui precariis orationibus suis Clarensium[4] vel ignescentes iras ab dura totiens opinione pacavit. Ab illo tu nunc barbaris feris atrocior, tu sanguinem exorbentibus Scythis[5] immanior, tu inexorabilior Acheronte refugis.* Quis crederet quod illius tam frequentibus litteris totque votis apprecatus ab tam adjurata* duritie tacendi non ultro potueris, non arte ulla ullisve precibus avelli, quasi gloriae tuae repositionem in amici contemptu fundaveris humanitatem exutus? Quare si secus est quam auguror, si supplicantium tibi natorum dulci unquam misericordia moveris ad hoc tandem scribendi genus, per eas ego te preces humaniter perque illud orandi numen obtestor, quibus Thrax vates ille Orpheus lenibus lyrae modulis Euridicen ad usque saltem apertas fauces inferni subvexit. Vale pridie Chal. Januarias.

VIII. MICHAELI BAETO CLARENSI PHYSICO LAURA CERETE. S.[1]

(Vt, f. 15r–15v; Ve, f. 29r–29v)

Video in notatos in me planetarum aspectus quorsum tendat tua illa suspicio, qua videris arbitrari id me a nescio quo ephemeride sumpsisse. Sumpsi (non infitior) a majoribus nostris hoc quantulum in me doctrinae situm est. Nec spreverim tamen propterea vel astrologorum minimum, cum sim ipsa[2] vel totula propter illos, tanquam inter proceras arbores tenue virgultum, ac inter canes Alexandri lepuscula.[3] Licet a Phoebi atque Daphnes[4] certo pignore lauro Laurae sortita sim nomen, non ut sub nomine, sed sub virtute vivam aeterna, neque ut fulminantem dei dextram effugiam, sed illi summa cum felicitate serviam ancilla, qui pro terrenis fragilibusque bonis et gentilium theologiae vates et victores gentium Caesares myrto lauroque donavit.[5] Vide nunc ipse tu, qui oculatissimus es, si tuus quisquis ille liber est, quem putas mihi ducem ad sidera, haec ista quae subiciam pro chirographi prioris declaratione docuerit. Metita sum igitur diei quarti Julii vigesimam horam,[6] sub qua (si memini) a leone ad virginem luna meabat a Saturno jam per Zodiaci gradus nonaginta distracta et ab Jove retrogrado atque directo Marte gradibus centum quasi viginti. Nunc in huiusmet positionis apertiore doctrina sis monitus, quod tunc quamvis Juppiter in quarta parte circuli generaret amicitiam bonae fortunae, in majore tamen odio flagrabat eadem dimensio bellici orientalisque Martis ad lunam. Sed maximum virus a mala fortuna occidentalis Saturni fluebat ad omnia maxime rerum discrimina purgatoriumque summendum, tum vel iter ingrediendum adeundosque reges. Tunc enim meridionalis virgo directa, duabus horis aequalibus, altius ascenderat. Luna vero in qualitate tenebrose et feminino sexu adhuc migrabat impedimenta viae combustae, soli novem fere gradibus praecedendo vicina, et erat jam in sexta domo cadente figurae caelestis in casuque Veneris nec procul ab exaltatione Mercurii. Erat autem concors frigidi et sicci complexio inter melancolicam triplicitatem signi atque Saturni retrogradi, ubi Algaphar stella fixa sub arctico coeperat aperire se nobis. Neque enim est in judiciis fixorum posthabenda cognitio. Tu illius curam habe atque vale. Pridie nonas Julias.

IX. SILVESTRO CERETE FRATER THOMAS MEDIOLANENSIS OR. PREDICATORUM S.[1]

(Vt, f. 38v–40v)

Mirabar prodiga praecipitive cum sub adolescentia lasciviens divagarer, unde avarus pecunia non impletur, nunquam rapiendi anxietatibus vel lassescat. Plagis teneor, quas damnabam. Praepedita namque quamquam ardentis avari atria quaquecircum sint argentis luxurientque annonis horrea et auro marsupia discindantur, edaci tamen haud ideo fit animae satis. Vorax adhuc esuriens est voluptas, et modo vacua est (inquam) ambitiosae gula voluntatis. Perennis namque anima, cum scalenonicam* utpote trinitatis plasma imaginem praefiguret interminataque illius definiatur esse capacitas, perfugax vero sphaerica†m†que ac vix ulla prorsus machina sit universi, ut actutum quidem defluant quaecumque caelorum claudi ambitu concernuntur. Quando implere tota illam creatura sufficiat, si nulla tripyrami* ad sphaeram ratio, si ne ulla infiniti commensuratio est ad finitum? Verum et rationali tradunt appetitu nihil esse liberius, qui consummatum naturaliter in bonum pronus – statum (inquam) optimorum congregatione perfectum – ad omnia proinde anhelat orbatum* ipse judicio quibuscumque mentis oculus inesse dictaverit appetibilis rationem. Ferturque in ea semper ardentius, quae cum eminentioris sub facie bonitatis offerantur arduiora sint obtentu. Optimis namque votis frustrari non patitur ambitio libertatis. Magnipendere hinc lapsa discimus, quae possessa olim in tuto licet aptiora vix vel advertere dignabamur. Quaecumque enim ad vota praesto nobis adesse conspicimus, jamque securi non formidamus amittere, non satis alliciunt appetitum, sane cuius nusquam libertati obsistere videantur. Insequimur autem plenis enixius votis absentia nitimurque semper in vetitum, ut noxia quoque inardescere propterea nonnumquam sentiamur.* Affectantur et ea propter conducentium recentiora semper avidius, duriusque desperata discrutiant, atque omnis ideo raptim ducitur oblectatio subvolasse. Quippe qui expetiti expectatique longius, aut necdum parta sit, aut acta mox comperierit et libertas. Hac ratione grandia locupletiores ambiunt, cum parcioribus sibi se quoscumque egestas premit saturandos esse mentiantur. Qui hi quidem excelsa quaeque ausint jam sperare, cum et tenuissima infimorum prope superent facultatem, quibus et ipsis ideo tamen obtentulum et spem ampliat et appetitum. Cum ergo in bonum creatis quibusque pronitas innascatur, appetanturque potiora (non ab re) semper ardentius, pertinacissima duntaxat in tenacitate otiosaque in attencendarum* infrugi[2] rerum sepultura exhorrescere satius avaritia decernatur. Rapiunt namque et dilapidator et avarus. Ardent et liberalis divitias et magnificus. Ast cum hi quidem quas* vel plurimis utiliter velint esse communes, plane qui harum effusione delectantur, solus has tenax universo perditas erugini occultat tineisque frustandas. Inebriasti me itaque mi Silvester fateor, sed salis poculo, pretiatissimi[s]que me muneribus perditasti, sed quibus ea inest insatietas, ut nulla eorum mensura, nulla quanta sit copia prae affectus nimietate mihi sufficere videatur. Excitasti concupiscentias in me, ac velut qui optatissimum diu ex insperato tenuerim agnitione quidem exarsi satis, altius et obtentu. Jam nil satis mihi esse sentio, quod lacteo ex illo fonte suavius emanasse contigerit, ubi recentius quicquam, quicquid id est, norim scaturisse. Neque ideo avarus esse censear. Sane cui ne vilescere quidem obtenta jam possint, nec otiosa marcescere mecum aut sepulta quaecumque optata olim ardentius. Conflagrans me jam sperare jubet ipsa cupiditas. Legi itaque et multa quidem animi jucunditate ex gratissimo muneris* nostri Felicis epistolam, in qua quercu ipse rigidior, barbaris atrocior feris et exorbentibus quoque sanguinem Scythis immanior ac ipso denique inexorabilior concrepatus est Acheronte.[3] Securae sentio haec amicitiae sunt, cum inopinabilia, non decipulas parent, et praedilectis impossibilia excandescentes imprecemur. Nam couterinam ingenuis peculiarius puellis humanitatem ac mansuetudinem innasci quis nesciat? Quales namque Felix in alia ejus epistola laudes quaeve praeconia consequatur? Dum cordiali quoque ipsa mentis amaritudine perlanguens haud ab re quidem dirius angeretur, sanguinoso intimius telo saucia si jam non meminerit Felix releg†isc†at. Librato in hac stilo internaque profundius meditatione mortis examinat et necessitatem et causas, uti et his flendum potius consulto ac religiose nimis asseverat, qui longiore sub hac infelicioris vitae molestia contorquentur. Flosculis conferta est, luctuosa licet, epistola consolaminibusque perfragrans, quae et lugenda instruit non fletu sed ratione superari.[4] Et mortalius (quam scite) vulnus memorat quod amor quam quod dolor incussit. In alia suorum perpulchre studiorum initia litterarumque amorem pensatis hercle sensibus aperit interfusis. Ceterum industriam ad Sigismundum epistolam quis congruis valeat praeconiis coaequare? Quid in ea dilectius magis admirer? Plane cuius et inventionum subtilitas et sollertia confutandi et narrationum series efficatiaque sermonis et sententiarum gravitas, et mellifluae sub eloquentiae gratia proprietas terminorum et congruentia denique coaptatioque ea verborum est, ut et syllabae et ipsa quoque resonent fragrantius elementa.[5] Felix palliolum quod trimestris arte lucubrationis, geometrica dimensione dinumerationeque harmonica Penelope isthaec nova contexuit, Babylonicae nimis Lucretiae invidiosum Emiliaeque Amazoni producentem oculos, quarum inferiore altera Federicum Augustum, altera victorem Theseum tentorio placavere.[6] Vidi et grata satis curiositate, quam apte (ut agi proelium ante oculos ponat) consertas enarret Sansoverino[7] Teutonum manus apud Athesim.[8] Diffusa utrinque agmina resarcitasque acies et versas rursum copias demersosque tandem infelices Atesi cuneos Italorum atque utriusque postremo excidium exercitus suspensa intentius fervidae mentis expectatione demirabar. Atqui quid et de asinariis ultra jam funeralibus loquar?[9] Quid fucato de ornatus muliebris apparatu?[10] Quid caelorum indagationes memorem,[11] quid herbarum peritiam?[12] Quid historias figmentaque recensuerim ac Tartareos manes?[13] Obstupui attonitus (fateor) ut mihi me somnio submentirer illudi. Quid puellae huic mansit incognitum? Quid fecunda illius ingenia non perspectius agnoverint? Quid non illius ferax sollertia vestigarit? Quid illi abditum natura occuluit, aut quos non lustravit haec auctores? Tot itaque tantisque jam illius epistolis ebrius gyro praecepsque ac vertiginosus, ut ipso quoque jam halitu stupida mens occupetur, ardeo sitiens, usque dum quicquid pretiatissimi liquoris validum hoc torcular exprimat epotarim.[14] Mereatur ergo mea in te fides amicorum observandissime. Impetret apud se calens hic meus in eam affectus observatioque singularis, ut epistolare illius volumen vel tribus diebus mihi mansurum accipiam,[15] quod innumeris florum splendoribus illustre, variis conspersum undique coloribus omnique redolens fragrantia pigmentorum modulante ab illa Orphei lyra, ipse tu significaveras et ipsa meminit enodatum. Sis mihi obsecro tantae huius genitae tuae (si salva ejus gratia) in operibus liberalis, cuius ipse me dignitatibus incredibilique stupidum excellentiae subdidisti.[16] Ego enim quamquam exteriorem illius hominem haud parvi arbitrer (quis namque tanto dignam habitatore non magni faciat mansionem?), rapior tamen ad intima prorsus. Quippe qua* sentio rarissimis est communis, si tamen alteram solaris uspiam radius intuetur. Huic astronomus Petrarcha[17] reor si non et prophetes longius arridens aliena sub specie cantitabat. Quam et intuitus est Lynceus,[18] et celsa caelorum advolitatione prospectavit. Felices Musas tali hac tantaque recentius alunna depromendas. Verum o quam feliciorem jam atque universo felicius ablactarent. Grandis haec aquila quo usque matris praeda pascitur aut venatur aticulum?* Usque quo ad upupulam volitat, aut insequitur carduelos? Quamdiu inquam franguli laudulaeque capitur vocibus, aut philomenae* modulationibus abducitur? Quoadusque divam hanc phoenicem solares ardentius radii non inflammant? Quae illi jam picae commercia sunt aut pavonis? Memoret vel Hieronymi plagas. Quid (proh dolor) caecam nesciamque virtutis hanc usque in aetatum scoriam expressa haec Palladis imago, improvida satis inertique fatorum sorte prolapsa est, cum nec Magdalena†e† Christo[19] nec Petro Dorcas,[20] non Drusiana Joanni,[21] non Hieronymo Paula foret aut Eustochium,[22] non vel Scolastica fieret Benedicto?[23] O si illa hanc tempora cognovissent, aut sanctorum quispiam serior nascebatur. Atqui non viat nobiscum Christus hodie; nullus hoc tempore Ambrosius, Macharii[24] cecidere, abest Augustinus, periit his diebus Antonius[25] omnis, et quisque postremo a nobis tempestate hac Hieronymus evolavit. Ceterum quid agimus, mi Silvester? Quales excusamus excusationes in peccatis? Nonne in suis praefati nobiscum operibus quotidie si volumus conversantur? Illae raros et quidem raro intuebantur, venerabantur, totisque nitebantur conatibus imitari. Quos et intuebantur homines, et peccabiles agnoscebant. Jam vero in nostris hi sunt mentibus, et plurimi quidem et longe digniores, utpote qui adepti palmas, ob egregia illorum et post vitae cursum facinora, ab universo jam profusius honorantur. Quos ergo tantos veneramur ac laudamus, quid non et amamus et contendimus imitari? Quid ab redeunte illo nobili homine praestolamur, qui regionem abiens in longinquam regnum sibi mox rediturus accepit?[26] Tantumne talentum hoccine auri purgatissimi pondo tradidit, ut florea duntaxat commercemur? Ignosce obsecro, et Laura pariter indulgeat. Comedit namque me zelus dei, in quo vale semper atque illa confortetur et valeat. Ac paucis modis decantatum illa somnium et meditari secum dignetur et attendere. vii Idus Octobris. 1487[27]

Pascebat jam Phoebus equos; jam clauserat orbem
Grata quies, non opta* dabat florecalia Taurus.[28]
Lapsus erat quo Libra[29] pares pensaverat horas.
Calcabat noxque atra diem, cum codice clauso
Sternileum[30] pulsata flagris rubra terga fovebant.
Huc variis jactata diu mens abvia, languens
Torpuerat. Jam lenta cadens Proserpina nostros
Lustrarat praecurva pedes, jamque improbus algens
Altius expansos somnus religaverat artus.
Ecce, procul, non pulsa noto, nullisque fatiscens
remis,[31] at excelso superans quoque sidera rostro,
Innumeris radians gemmis auroque corusca,
Ingens visa mihi volitans super aequora puppis
Laurus erat malus altus ea, mastrincula quercus[32]
Firmabatque utrumque calibs, calibesque tuentur.
Aspicio. En rapidus stridensque per aequora perflat
Aquilo, et horrendos versat per inania fluctus.
Obduxit nox atra polum, jamque emicat aether
Ignibus: ecce vorax puppem subsorbet hiatus.
Expaveo. Vox alta tonat: convellite laurum.

x. LAURAE CERETAE FRATER THOMAS MEDIOLANENSIS OR. PRAEDICATORUM S.[1]

(Vt f. 41v–42v)

Operosa me desudatione melliflua satis, sed et pontica atque acrior epistola tua reddidit expeditum. At mordax Boniphatii urentius[2] haud obaudum* sanguinaria sauciavit, quam expetito (plane nimis) ipsa libello tuo, ceu candentia inter lilia et fragrantes rosas, sed et juxta feniculum, pullulantiaque subter dumeta et urticulas anguem callidius abdidisti. Melliflua inquam apis instar est et pontica,[3] quae fusa quidem in mellis redundantia subtectans aculeum, sale etiam nititur fel condire, cuique praesidi inter suavitatem lactis penetratior non desit agreste acuitas mordicatioque aceti. Et cum vaporatio uberius incalescat pigmentorum, sentitur nihilominus et sinapis. Tuae tamen indignat vinculae tua* intelligo remissius quam par erat inurere videbatur, atque ideo canis tibi coassumptus est longe mordacior. Impudens ille oblatrator inquam, qui in magistro Benedicto sacro praedicatorum ordini quasi spumans aper insultat. At qui probatissimam divi Dominici institutionem summis effert seductus ille praeconiis, dum impugnat ipsoque confoditur veruto fremens quod impingit. Sed num naturali quoque ac sapientiae, quin et revelatae oratorios anteponere fucos ausu temerario vesanus aggreditur? Pestilentem igitur hanc blasphemamque deliri nebulonis crocitationem dedisti ad me tuis insertam, plane ut quod pro ingenua animi generositate puellarique mansuetudine ipsa non audebas, ferina id saltem immanitate ipsa subridens consequaris diroque me furiosi digladies mucrone crudelius, quem cruentare pavidula verearis. Ignosce clipeo soror pharetrata. Sauciae ordo mentis est nescisse ordinem, flammivomasque exsufflare praecipitantius voces quas urget passio, non quales metiatur modestia ratiove dictarit. Non sum prorsus (fateor) ab homine destitutus. Sic autem et agnula* mordes? Sane hoc (inquis) impar sibi argumentum est, neque accusatoria haec ratio ea est, quae me ream indefensamque perstringat. Immo niterer via retrorsa (subdis), si morem tibi gererem, qui ex optato, non ex sententia mihi consulis. Impexum ego me balbiticulumque abs te impetitus ultro deferebam. Sane cui haec usque fuerint ligustra[4] contemptui, quae quisquis inani dierum attritione pomposaque inflatior elaboratione persequitur, sero sibi se discit esse delusum. Paralogus[5] vero a puella* non videbar quia lingua floreat increpandus, quippe qui terquinos ante annos et syllogizare et demonstrare docui et paralogismos abdicare. Verum de ruditate adhuc sola carpebar ingenii atque ignorantia crassiore. Jam vero et proditorem iratior criminaris, dum retrorsam seducens in viam ex optato accusor infidus non ex sententia tibi consulere. Demiror satis ubi ea te infausta nimis in epistola scite adeo causeris serioque morderi, quaeve auditu tibi gravia eo usque legeris aut infesta, aut unde subdola isthic insidiosaque consilia subnotaris, ut in me tantillum licet, tui tamen observantissimum tam dire impingens, atque omni seposita generosae mentis benignitate tam inhumaniter invecta conteris. Est quidem apud me adhuc infelicis illius epistolae praelitura,[6] quam qui tuae conferat, sinistrae distortaeque interpretationi tuae crimen hoc ascribet. Sed conjecisti forsan tibi conscia, ut pote ex ignorantia non delinquens, unde digna sis reprehendi. Paralogum ergo dolosumque consulem et omnium doctiorem vocas et tibi deligis praeceptorem? At neque oratoria haec tura nos odoramus, plane quae venabaris ipsa conjicio. Sic tibi tu videris verba singultire, sic describere fumo chartas, ut non nisi censore no[ve]ris calamo quicquid ipsa non edideris oppugnare? Quis fucata in hac humilitate tua ipsi tibi te submentiri liquido non agnoscat, dum nullius verita vires ingenii, quasi nullius arti gratiaeve secunda, quando et una cuiusque praeimpar facundiae tuae hos litteraturae quos strepitus vocas ac sensus tenues, caracterizatos elementatim[7] ad omnes liberius orbe populos, oratores, philosophos, ac eruditissimos quosque disseminare latius, atque universorum audeas judicio securior produxisse quasi leo quae ad nullius paveas occursum? Humilitade dico io.* Insidiosa clariorem subinfitiari gratiam consuevit hypocrisis, aperireque abditam latentius, aut et impartam, ut favorem hinc sibi atque hinc praeconiaque tumidior commercetur, dum et hac attolli virtute ambiens et vult pariter humilitas praedicari. Fiat-que ut dum simulato rubore perspectum dei munus depositis in commendatione sui oculis diffitetur, possidere indubitanter et virtutem qua inanis est censeatur. Sed cervum saltu tritum est comprobari. Testea quam solida sint fornacis flamma denuntiat. Et namque si (ut portendis) ipsa de te sentis humilia, quid ab dilectoribus tuis in levissima re commonita sic ageris in furorem, cum gravius ipsa te subaccuses? Est qui nequiter se humiliat (inquit sapiens) qui cum impatientissime id ab alio audiat furens, in quo seipsum ipse saepius ultro criminatur, monstrat apertius qualem voci propriae tum cupiat fidem adhiberi. Sed non impinguet caput tuum soror oleum peccatoris. Inspira olim itaque pausatius soror, et gregatos ex corde capinosos[8] agitatis extende folliculis. Complana frontem. Acumen linguae amputa. Obtunde vel calamum, soror amantissima, modestiaeque lima moderare. Et nobis putasti spicula facesque deesse? Verum calibea* es. Quis nexea* in te tela, quid vel flammigerum Medeae[9] pallium posse reformidem? Quid letiocula* in te Annibalis testea moliantur? Laureas namque virulenta baccas usquequaque profugiunt, et lauro cerrisque veneficia dissolvuntur. Cereta salutans salus. Saluti infestum nihil est, nihil insalubre. Vale in domino. Pridie nonas Novembres.

XI. LAURAE CERETE FRATER THOMAS MEDIOLANENSIS ORDINIS PRAEDICATORUM S.[1]

(Vt, f. 43v–47r)

Escandescentia* mellicantium agmina nostras* haud falso vindex epistola tua figurabat, et (nanque non peccantes irascimur, melle dulcescentes caritatis internae) et spinosas (emphatica quanquam) penitus non mentitur. (Verba etenim sapientum stimuli, et quasi clavi in altum defixi). Iratius vero apum examen, ultrice dum nostras* indignatior orditu proclamas apertius, sola te jam tutabitur abusio vel hyperboles excusabit. Insueta mihi alienaque ac extranea prorsus nequicquam contendis recenter ascribere. Sive namque ea mihi sit chystifellis[2] patens amplaque capacitas, quae fervidae nil colerae arteriarum sinat spiritibus admisceri, seu laxam tepentis cordis expansionem habes, non sufficiat, sopitusque calor inflammare, vel torpentes ignavo sensus obtusi, atque iners tepor effeminato absumat audaciam. Aut certe couterina me a natalibus mansuetudo eatenus obtinuerit abundantiave pietatis, ut infusae et artubus totum jam sibi me plenius vendicarint, nulla unquam vel irae me facies fecit ultorem. Dei haec largitio est munusque naturae, quod nequaquam propria mihi virtus actionesve pararunt. Absit itaque, ut hoc domini gratuitum, inditam hanc mihi ex cunis mititatem, tantae ad sororis injuriam destituisse primum videar. Cuius ante iratiora quoque ora et rinoceronthe* truculentiores mansuescere deceat, et obsequiosae prorsus humanitati subjacere. Ast si gregatos alvearii favos cereasque cellulas, cum hiematura frequentant examina contueri, audaces arcent horum accessus aculeis, quos et mella surripere, et quadrangulas congerere illorum mansiunculas. Et si ad extremum quoque metuant enecare, quis iratiora haec ideo rectus improbitet, cum et pares irrogatis ultiones inculpata tutella sanctio promulget canonum honestari? Si ergo rependens absque usura beneficium gratus non est, nec proinde sine faenore retorquens injuriam censetur ultor, quam immanius quisque beneficus lapidatur. Quid namque noster ille palearum ventilatus fascis ad integerrimum dominum genitorem tuum, praeter gratiam laudes tuaeque praeconia virtutis advexit?[3] Nisi hac te qu†a†eraris esse lacessitam,quod tanta indignum aquila esse diximus, acerrimo (inquam) fecundoque hoc ingenio tuo aviculas insequi.[4] Rhetoricen scilicet poesisque mellitis semper obvolvi reticulis. Plane cui natura contulit ab directo solis radio lumina non declinare, ut altissima et optent et sufficiant intueri. Nimis et Phoenice[5] indignum esse censuimus. Libera (inquam) imperatoriaque voluntate cum pica pavonibusque inire consortia, cum oblatratoribus ac elatis et mundanae addictis prorsus vanitati. Eo voluntas tua conflagret igne caritatis, quem supremi solis radius nititur inflammare. Obstupui (fateor) tanti fulgoris carbunculum solis irradiare noctivolis. Expavi et luto infossum hoc margaritum scintillante adeo splendescere claritate. Jucunda mirabundus amaritudine perlegeram scripta tua captus in ecstasim, cum ne satis indicarem suspensus animo, utrum ne laudanda fores potius an carpenda. De tanto quidem invento thesauro exultabam. Angebat me tam prodiga infrugalisque illius effusio, ut nequiverim (fateor) gaudens admirans dolensque non clamare: heu quid tanti tanta perditio. Speraveram autem ingenuae mentis tuae benignitati non esse infestum, nec odiosum hoc tibi (ut scribis) virus esse. Tua me patiebatur humanitas arbitrari, quod audaciunculas in me tuas non sum veritus tui amantior moderari. Quid tibi soror amantissima sum suspectus? Non ego coniventibus in te feror Eusebii oculis aut Cassandrae.[6] Nihil te mihi praeter virtutis tuae splendorem innotuit, quae laurae omnifariam dispergere jam nomen auditur ac longius quaque personare.[7] Pretiosus mihi nimis quo rarior quidem in adolescentula,[8] et pro foribus quidem relicta semel, cum et vixdum suppetere viro videreris,[9] almus iste turturis caelibatus, digna et integrior inviolataque in libertate opinio, et clara sub natalium generositate affluentiaque fortunarum humanitas. Et lautior et inter mensas testis parsimoniae gracilitas macilentiaque membrorum, et juges postremo inter domesticae at familiaris curae sollicitudines, vigil haec studiorum instantia conatusque ad altiora intentior semper semperque recentior. Quae nisi praematuras purpura operari genas tuas intuear flavoque silvestrium liliorum rubore candentia suspicer laudata coram ora jam vestiri, abundantiore mihi et jejunio posthac fuerant* oratione prosequenda. Atqui num ideo neque maculam in te rear esse neque rugam? Perfecti nusquam nisi in caelo sunt. Laterem quisquis contenderit abluere delirabit, et lunae iratior nequicquam canis allatrat. Levem autem ab margarito pulverulam sincerus festinat amator abigere, et primam ex auro rubiginem sagax ocius curator abradit. Audi exoro pensatior monita caritatis. Majora sane laudibus nostris orata tua sunt, sed vaporare utrumque sentiuntur oratoriumque nescio quid grandius ostentare. Venatur oratoria praeconium, cuius peculiariter indignatio consuevit, quaecumque propria aestimatione inferiora parcior vel fidelis laudator obtulerit, parvipensiones, si non vel opprobria computare. Adeo sibi grandet orator, cuius aures ad propriam prurientes linguae facundiam, pavonumque oculi, maturior gestus, incessus gravior atque undivagus, amplus pretiosiorque vestitus atque togatior admirabilem se cunctis arbitrari hunc monstrant, quorum decapuciationes ambit et praestolatur. Sic oppidanus consul forsan post hebdomadae fluviales potus aratrique sudores creatus quidem sub circuli signo in die solis hilarior, cum sub plateae ulmo stipitis in promontorio eminentior, tineato affatim pandulfeo superbus apice, si non carmagnoleo[10] aut pellito evenit, rugatissimaque zodiatice obtectus dissarcita[11] divisatius equina ut contingit opertura, Bernabovis reliquia forsan aut Bracii, plane cui dependula cadunt semicinctia circum laceraeque frappae,* quanque corrosum (stapedile[12] olim) lumbare obvolvit incomptius, cuius ferrugineam quidem fibulam, transversatus pro stumbulo[13] rubiginosus retentat clavus. Rudi circumstipatum se caterva, patulis ad se faucibus appensa prospectarit. Ipsum se surrigens in articulos, ac tumentius lustrans stupebundam[14] ad se (pavonis instar) inertis vulgi nititur expectationem intentosque oculos convocare. Alternos tum violentius extentans tibiones,[15] follicantes profert Sfortiadas.[16] Quae dispatulae quidem in subimo,[17] suffectisque ac ferratis superfusae calceis hos verrunt in incessu. Supplexa[18] tum denique proceraliter cinctorio callosa ustaque solibus utrinque manu, protractoque setis densiore supercilio, sic bubo gracitat,* stolidum circumagens caput. "Hoc me audite consulem ignavi compotenque rationis. Quis namque vobis ego sum? Aut quanta me nosce[re] posseque putatis?" Producit tum depopulationes avitas ordine nullo gestaque majorum et inflexibili obesaque lingua priscas praepostero penurias gurgitatim excreans narrat. Ac lunae aggressus alternamenta fracte syncopansque disserere, ac saepe idem repetens, quasi Ptolomeum Catonemque sibi se aut Plinium a nemine interceptus arbitretur.[19] Ad patris tandem boumque funebria largius quidem flectitans deducit historiam demum et aselli, ut grandiora trutinantem inter arvorum patres aselli mox recordatio reddiderit infelicem.[20] Qui si ranarum forte distracturus excoriata crura ingreditur civitatem, aut inde Gangen forsitan evecturus, jam quemque Dominum vocat. Pavibundusque assuitur parieti, ac cedens terga de capuciatus[21] operitur. Itidem et solius excultor linguae, sonora quidem voce in vulgo gregibusve probucinans puerorum, si demonstratorem, sed vel dialecticum fortassis offenderit, suas tum primo discit vesicas scientiae nomen non mereri. At vero quantillum hoc est, quod et hi se scire ausint confiteri, quos vulgatior opinio censet esse doctissimos. Hoc nanque dicimur scire, cuius unanquamque limpidius intuemur causam atque inevitabiliter novimus ita causare.* Est ergo scientia lumen et demonstrationis virtute intellectui impressum, quo deductae quidem conclusionis clare videt intellectus veritatem. Demonstratio quid sit et ex quibus, ex Posterioribus fateor Analecticis[22] legi. Quid autem aliquando viderim esse demonstratum, mens non habet. Et nanque non est absque illius definitione demonstratio cui passio inesse monstranda est. Non est autem definitio absque propria natura convertibilique differentia. Quam cuius vel entis minimi rogo cognoscimus? Quid nobis eousque apertum sentiamus, cuius nos nobis videamur aptitudines perspexisse? Quod si quam ex actu forte deducimus, quis rerum differentias, a quibus nascuntur propria, vel doctissimus perscrutetur? Incorporeorumne an incorrupti corporis aut eorum forte, quae caelorum rotatio destruit incessanter? Illa non attingimus. Huius pro nihilo est quod annosissimis jam sensuum deductionibus et credere nos oportet. Quid itaque de his putemus quae semper altera ex incognitis supra causis pendent, quibus et omnimode* subducuntur?[23] Sane hoc duntaxat didicit, qui tempora non inaniter attrivit studiorum, quod nihil sciat. Doctior est quicunque propriam apertius nescientiam intuetur. At scioli cum ignorantiae caligini profundius immergimur, quod superficialia quidem lambentes, interius nihil perscrutemur, omnia nobis nos applaudimus ebibisse. Hinc grande aliquid nobis nos esse submentimur, qui et ceteras quasque contemptui ducimus disciplinas. Carpimus et incognita, edita mordemus aliorum semper ac depravamus. Hanc igitur tibi metuens oratoriae caliginem cordialissima soror irrepere (gignunt namque saepius iterati actus habitum) redditus ab caritatis zelo forsan audacior, quicquid attolli in tuis videretur, fraterna dilectione cordeque ardenti fidelis censor obtundebam. Quam pretiosum scientiae ornamentum, quam decorum virtutis monile, quam gloriosum celsitudinis est margaritum humilitas. Tu oratoriam impretiabilis huius vocalis novercam si dederis ancillari, sed vel sociam prudentissima copularis, utpote quae fecundo uberius calice ad satietatem amplissimoque stomaco jam rhetoricen epotasti, beatam et te generationes omnis post domini genitricem proclamabunt. Sane cuius possessione virtutis potissimum, cum spiritu dei exundans, omnis sublimius decorata fuerit et excellentia virtutis et gratiae. Ipsa se Maria virgo et domini matrem intelligit et beatam se prophetavit ab universo fore praedicandam. Haec solidum spiritualis aedificii fundamentum ab immo extruit ad empyreum usque parietes. Non evagatur. Despicit numquam. Nunquam ad inferiora reflectitur, sed fixo semper intuitu intendit in deum, usque dum comprehendat. Haec virtutum custos est, gratiae inventrix, reparatio prolapsorum, rubricatae sceleribus animae dealbatio, tutissima mentis requies, cordis jubilus, exaltatio angelorum, mansio denique ac thronus Dei. Jam vero resilientia sustine missilia soror, sed sanguine apud vos intincta caritatis. Caritas patiens est, benigna est, omnia sustinet, congaudet autem veritati. Jam tuas quaeso, socialiter evolvamus. Indagemur qualia isthic humilitatis florea delitescant. Si objurgatoria cum nec novisti abrupta vaditare[24] necdum calamos emisti (ut scribis) absinthia distillantes, nulla te genera fugiunt objurgandi, nullaque usquam tui calami vacant specie napellorum.[25] Quid cum et hos tibi tu videbere calamos assumpsisse? Probant epistolae tuae quam spatioso jam itinere vix hodie incipiens in hac recriminandi provincia cursitaris. Sin pervolitans dixerim potius, bravio* jam finitima sis objurgandi. Hinc sentio quanta in me modestia frenationeque volentem compescueris animum et trisulcos humanitate calamos te ipsa fortior ad me modereris. Moles sunt, qui non penitus urticosi sunt aut mordaces. Sed nostrum non fuit qualia responderes. Quantique abs te parvuli penderemur. Si nomen apud te venabamur atque praeconia, utique thymiamata spargebamus oratores, turaque adolebamus, unde ad nos congesta fecundius refunderentur atque confluerent. Absit ut quia palpuli celebremur. Letaris omnibus invidum laurae nomen surrexisse. Et mihi? Surrexisse inquis. Jam? Effecisse id censes veritatem, ut vulgo scripta tua displiceant. Et nobis ergo? Nos quoque inter hos? Cui autem nisi male sibi conscio displicere veritas possit? Quis furor (oi) te Laura focat?* Quam sentit Agaven Pentheus? Heu quae non vel Laurea corda revelas Fama fugax? Quae non vel ferrea pectora mulces Fama levis? Quae non quercinea viscera palpas Fama loquax nomenque volans laudumque cupido. Quae virtus tibi tua fuit? Quae claustra? Quod antrum? Herostrato[26] itaque tuae me sentio famosiorem esse †pro†bucinant, qui apprime scelestus facinorumque minera,* supremae licet ignaviae, effreni tamen ambitionis cupiditate accensus, edacique peraestuans livoris incendio, qua nocte Philippo Alexandrum[27] illegalis consors enixa est, nomen et ipse inter illustres praestantior accepturus, Ephesiae fanum Lucinae incendit, quod quidem insigne orbis trecentorum sudoribus annorum universaque ferebatur Asiae manu surrexisee. Sacris ille focis vel nomen acquisiit. Ego (ut censes) splendoris tui obnubilatione[28] nomen amiserim. Hic surrexit ex facinore non vulgaris. Ego vulgi gregibus exhibitione congeror pietatis. Sua illi parvipensio fuit infesta, mihi gloria tua intolerabilis erit. Quo mihi et bestia immanior Nero conferatur, qui cum Agrippinae matris truculentus viscera rimaretur, cuius doloso facinore (boletis namque Claudium ipsa consumpserat) ipse Nero tyrannabat imperium, accersito aestuans haustu torvus epotavit? Is matri sed homicidae vitam abstulit. Ego angelicae sororis dum livore rumpor, pretiosiorem vita non desisto nominis gloriam subneruare. Ille caedes atque incendia ob nominis ambitum perpetravit. Ego innoxiae sororis ardens exsufflare gloriam, proprium nil curaverim nomen ipse lacerari. Sic? Et rogas soror an summis crediderim e labiis tua tibi verba fluxisse.[29] Si haec tibi mox e labiorum ultimis sponteque deciderent, qualia ex cordis librata penetralibus advertero fulminari? Interiore pervolans ex tormentarii abdito sphaera silicea diruit altius ac dilacerat, horrendiusve subvertit, tametsi feminae plus laudis ferre sollertia quam consilium videatur? Et nostra tamen verba non nescias rationis ab trutina examinari primum bovinoque pedetentim lasso tandem incessu procedere, formidolosa semper et quaque circumspectantia quorsum quandove tendatur. Non sum (fateor) aut ingenio tibi aut sollertia compar[30] acrimoniaque scribendi. Sed plurimos ab nimium aestu et vulpes contuentur. Saepius namque et callidiores cum versutos introrsum in cogitatus rapti, advocatam menti prorsus animam concentrant sua intentius meditantem, simpliciorum ab captiunculis. Dum superficialius conamina illorum pensant incurii, ex insperato supplantantur. Sic scachorum[31] colludiis dimicantes, inopinatis crebro angustiis cohibentur. Sane qui dum rapinis, fuso agmine divagantur avidius, aut regi obsidionem infestius moliuntur, aut certant oppugnare arces, vel cruenti trucidare militiam. Machinanturque in consules, ac peditum crassantes in sanguine caedibus debacchantur, et reginam denique dehonestare nil veriti aggrediuntur immanes decolare, ipsi ex adverso capiuntur incauti, ut quadruplicatae medius areae rex hostili quidem circumstipatus agmine nulloque vallatus praesidio, dum laxatur in praedam omnis exercitus, vili a pedite captivus audiat. Scaccho mato di pedone nel mezo tavolerio.* Nec secus gladiarii actitantes quidem agilius dum fervore peraestuantes feriendi, vulnus hostis attentius observant quam gladium ingesti apertius; crebro sauciantur infelices. Tecum est mens tua (memoras) quae hos te suadeat arguere, quos vel toto admiseris pectore cariores. Scite ac sancte. Sed et dilectoribus tuis id ipsum ascribito. Quid tui me, quaeso, invidum subnotavit? Tantin* tibi tu, aut eousque tibi sum gogulus,[32] ut ipsa, cui ego qui possim invidere? Quid Caesaris aut Pompei elatam jam nunc arrogantiam crimineris quorum hic superiorem hic vel comparem ferre non potuit? Loquitur ad cor meum saepe peregrinus. Si nec homines (inquit) nec nostra deus ipse scelera sit agniturus, si nec poenam pro facinore nec infamiam vereamur, certe ipsa horret excellentia spiritus. Conscientia reformidat, damnat synderesis. Aspernatur et corporis harmonia, et ipsa honestatis justitiaeque innata mentibus dilectio proclamitat abstinendum. Rosae tuae densa nimis at stipata spinarum maceria sepiuntur, manumque non nisi ferream patiuntur admittere, cum fracida ego cute sim ungueque inermis molliori. Frustra sentio inferiorum auro characterum, ab divite ingenio tuo, pretiosissima lucrosior faenera* praestolabar, qui pro pannosis sperarem ex orientalibus margaritas. Ad meam ergo mihi pacem est redeundum. Ubi laeta sub pauperie alter mus ruralis delitescam? Quemque inter grossiores epulas Phocion[33] consoletur, qui integer severusque immo et pertinax amator egestatis, cum per magnifica pauper Alexandri munera despexisset, adhortarenturque illum sui cariores ut vel cautior liberis pie prospiceret, qui illustrem patris gloriam sub despectiore adeo non essent rerum penuria defensuri, egregie dixit: Patris filios eadem teget casa idemque alet agellus. Alterorum vero nolim luxurias adaugere. Aversa haec te facie stomacantem contracto vultu labroque presso ac deducto nimbosius cilio indignatius lectitasse tua confestim silentia testabuntur. Vale viii Kal. Decembri.

XII. LAURAE CERETAE FRATER THOMAS MEDIOLANENSIS ORDINIS PRAEDICATORUM S.[1]

(Vt f. 48v–51r)

Inflammavit ora rigentia aestuantemque introrsus animum oratoria nimis et nostri generosius aculei vindex epistola tua consopivit. Quae spiritus quidem sitibundo in corde prae gaudii* multitudine congregatos, perculsam urentius mox in faciem synthomatico* impulsu profocavit,* ut meipsum nimis erubescens nusquamque latitans satis et mihi me satagerem anxius occultare. Digitari[2] me quaque suspicabar circumspectans, cunctorumque rebar subridere ocellos in me mitantius.* Et contracto quosque vultu verebar subsannanter in me ac provecto despectim labro sibilare, cum pictae industrius pennigeraeque affatim epistolae stupens facieque ignivomus vel primas quidem submurmurans plausulas pavidule[3] irreperem cunctinque oblitus halitum conjectarer. Nemini quidem imperspectam rebar intro mihi conscius cordis esse passionem, quam purpureae confusionis genae ultro apertiusque monstrarent. Hu†nc†cine igitur unae meae atque alterae tibi me nuntiarunt, cui palpula haec alludere deliramenta censueris conflatiliaque huiuscemodi adulamenta comprurire? Haeccine (inquam) vaporalia mihi ad te turibula incendebantur, sane unde stipatius ad me refusa conflagrarent, ut venari me nomen atque laudulas, cranevacuum[4] opinata fueris aucupari? Oratorias his praefumiga nares odoribus et turgentes horum vesicas ventosa hac expande fistula, quorum reflexus est semper intuitus, atque utinam et lynceus foret. Quorum sua vox et suas duntaxat implet rumoribus aures. Ast tantillus ego, si vel ullus, cui pro summa est sapientia, vel hodie cum sim annosior, nosce quam nihil sciam et quam sim nihil. Ei fucata hyperbole quid confundor potius abs te quam lauder? Ceterum etsi rubore legentis saepe facies incaluerit, defeceritque primum mens in seipsa confusior, scrutata tamen tua in his bonitas interius repensum largius caritate mihi cor ampliavit. Neque enim ideo tibi te censuerim soror esse mentitam, quod et ultima et prima sim commendatione tua satis inferior, sed cuius anima* oculos tanti tua me dilectio gratius obtulisset. Absit ut palpulam[5] ego te arbitrer assentari. Debeo proinde supra quod rependere sufficiam satis humanissimae menti tuae soror ingenua, quae ab caritatis tuae fulgoribus illustratum, etsi opacum in se sit, tibi tamen tuopte offertur in lumine radiosum. Solaris nusquam radius tenebras intuetur. Pulchrescit (trito aiunt) quodcumque id fuerit in amato. Honori nihil inglorium. Sentes dilectio flores facit, et naevos quoque speciosissima quaedam ornamenta zelantum cernere admirarique auspicia consueverunt. Concavo me reor in speculo propior mirabaris, cum reflexa ab procera puellariter imagine trepidares. Plurima jam rumor vix ul†l†ula dedit in caelos. Succrevere opinionibus apicula,* et sensum imaginatio rationemque quam saepius abillusit. Atqui eo ipse, si me in speculo absentior contempleris, tantillus confestim tibi offeror et eversus. Censebis ilico ac purgatiore liquido intueberis oculorum acie oratorios me nec postes quidem vidisse aliquando nec quaesisse, nempe quem vix eblesulum* adversa his satis et quidem indefesse studia possederint. Nullus me orandi scribendive nitor ornavit, nullius clarui gnarus oratoriae facultatis. Qui ne unam quidem Ciceronis oratiunculam aut me legisse memorem aut audisse. At nec rhetoricen* quando colores edidici vel praecepta, quem soli Seneca neposque Lucanus affectum satis fateor quantum bissenium indulgere pueritium* posset discipulum ex oratoribus ablactarunt. Verum et superingruentes secundo mox in septennio exterae sat ab his curae studiorum acriorque cultus ingenii heroica continuo angustosque congesta sub moralitate a†m†phorismos funditus abdicarunt. Illepidum eapropter oratoriaeque me artis jejunum non erubeo confiteri, quod frugaliores longe inter mensas si non ad satietatem quidem aut sufficientiam sum refectus; vel quotulas tamen micas avidius redundantiaque amoenitatibus fragmenta vel sapidius ipse degustarim. Quantillum in me est, hoc nullius omnino est artis vel initium. Sentitur autem ut dialectica, sic et rhetorica innasci, quandoquidem, sicut enuntiaria[6] conceptuum passionumque et affectuum est expressio rationalibus naturalis, ita et blandius emollire et commovere humilius et petulantius extorquere, provocare terrereque ac suadere agrestes quoque rusticuli apud nos docente nullo et gesta et confutationibus moliuntur. Sed et vivax plurimis effluxit ingenium innataque quibusdam pronitas, germen fermentumque ac radius quidam inest doctrinarum, ut quod assiduo ceteri studio jugique vix exercitatione nanciscuntur, naturae quodam impulsu illi acerrimeque sollertia rationis intime quidem et clarius velocissimeque conquirant. Horum ego longe nimis ab ingenio absum gratiaque doctrinae. Excitavit autem et in Cimone stertentem amentia sensum Iphigenia virgo.[7] Quae dum sorte quidem florea inter prata, meridiano solula somno, blandiore sub pomiferi umbra mulceretur, ex rudi despectoque ac stolido nebulone gratiorem Florentiae civem recreavit et jumentali reddidit ex dementia conspicuum visum, ut in clarissimum denique cunctisque honoratissimum repente patricium felicis illius virginis dilectio sibi bestiam transformaret. Quid dissentaneum quaeso, si tua recenter studia et nullis insimulanda criminibus aemulatio sopilentam hactenus inertiam desidemque torporem hodie mihi primum excusserint, ut tuae si virtutis nequeam culmen tantillus assequi, si plenis volitantem sinibus, altique profundiora felicius postergantem[8] nequiverim classem tuam conchula isthac resarcitaque remigulus[9] cymba[10] comprehendere, sequar tamen utcumque proficiens teque piculus deficientissime quanquam coner simiare? Ceterum si exundantis affectus tui contendero excessum in singulis annotare, excrescet video labor in volumen. Quem namque consumatae adeo virtutis norit aetas nostra vel saecula jam viderunt, qui tuis par esse laudibus censeatur aut tua haec possit praeconia coaequare? Cuius enim dilectioni tuae tenacior esse memoria sentiatur atque capacior? Quid Augustini, quid Deodati[11] aut Aquinatis Thomae ferventior tua isthaec magnipensio[12] aestimet ingenia valuisse? Dii meliores! Quibus te oculis ditarit natura benignior, qua mente, quibus ingenii viribus, ut in arida testa favos videas, quos nulla unquam examina labore s†c†edulo congregarint? Si rideor, rideo. Sed aestimo tu te soror in me contemplaris. Saciasti* et his denique perfectionis universae custodiam, quae vel una nobiscum soror amantissima convivere dignaretur. Cetera namque ornamenta sunt ingenii cui cum carnis onere liberius evolarit. Quaecumque aut synderesis dictet aut inducere sufficiat intellectus, nulla penitus deductione infusim ilico sunt aperta. Gloriosior vero haec sui contemptiva cunctisque celsior humilitas, quamquam caeca ab elatione indigno nimis ignaviae vocabulo nuncupetur. Una haec tamen est unius et veri praeceptoris disciplina. Discite a me, dominus inquit, quia mitis sum et humilis corde. Humilibus dat gratiam, qui humilia respicit, et alta a longe cognoscit. Hodie ira, furor, impatientia ultioque atque crudelitas audaciae ac strenuitatis nomina sortiuntur. Superbia generositas est animi, et ambitio magnificentiae claritatisque nominibus honora†n†tur. Cum ex adverso bonitas, benignitas, mansuetudo, humilitas, patientia, pietas ceteraque id genus et verae humanitatis ornamenta ingenuaeque mentis pronitates ab desidis putentur animi vilitate descendere obtusique accusentur sensus et insensibilis atque ignavae mentis infirmitates opprobriaque contemnantur. Has contra bestias lupis tigrideque atque ursis immaniores, ne vel grandioris animi leonibus conferantur, indignum satis est rationibus disceptare. Quippe qui humanitatem exuti, expertes et proinde rationis se se opus est fateantur. Sed homo (inquient) nobilissimus est creatorum. Cui non imperet? Quidni gloriam quaerat? Quid contra naturae donum libertatem subdi servireque glorietur? Vel corporum hoc dixissent. Quid si angelorum exercitibus militiaeque archangelorum infinitisque beatorum spirituum agminibus homo conferatur, quorum cum infimus magnanimis proportione naturam nostram excellentia perfectioneque praecellat, tantus est numerus, ut ne illi quidem universorum valeat sensibilium numerositas coaequari? Est fateor materialium homo excellentissimus conditorum,[13] sed veluti si mineralium terra immixti auri moles dignissima censeatur. Quid namque humano corpore videatur infirmius, quod exiguus quoque culex inquietat, inficit, exulcerat, occidit? Quid eo foedius, quid immundiore scatens undique abominatione? Quid stomachosa[14] horribilius putredine devitatur? Quid eo ipso, inquam, est turpius tantidemque pudendum? Sed hospite destituatur,[15] evanescat aurum, spiritus exsuffletur. Quid gleba erit hac horrendius aequeve terrificum? Homo itaque qua corpus est, qua corruptibilis est ex materiaque compactus, inter viliora quidem convincitur esse vilissimus. Qua vero immaterialis, plane et infimus ei locus ascribitur. Quippe quem (ut prefati sumus) incorporea quaeque numeroso exuperant ordine dignitatis. Humiliatio sane tua homo in medio tui est. Dignissimam tamen non dediscimus essentiam esse animam rationalem hominemque per ipsam, sed non nisi stola ornatus fulgeat nuptiali. Et namque dignior est diabolus per naturam. Quid autem est a gratia caritateque longius, quid est odibilius deo, superbia? Superbis resistit deus, qui alta a longe conspicit. Inde vero ad mortis compuncta memoriam, per singula ubiubi momenta, nostris hanc pervigil ipsa memoras cervicibus impendere, quam praecavere, non nisi is merito censendus est, qui hanc sibi et ubique et jugiter meminerit imminere. Aurorae post noctis caeca silentia, post adolescentiam senectae, mortisque post functionem hanc una est expectatio. Noctem non viderit qui nolit auroram,[16] juventutem ille nescierit, qui odit senium, noluerit vitam qui nolit mori. Nascentium mors est indistincta condicio. Oderit nasci qui mori nolit. Atqui quid hac juvet inter diaboli gladios angi diutius, ubi tot persecutiones animus quotidie patitur, tot periculis pectus urgetur, tot morbi, tot metus, tot curae, ut nullum videatur morte votum esse frequentius? Hebescunt hic sensus in dies, membra torquentur, defluunt ciborum instrumenta, contabescit corpus immobile, ut nobis ipsis quoque reddamur onerosi. Quid itaque nobis esse possit vitae brevitate jucundius, quid utilius, quid ardentius affectandum? Quid namque mors est, nisi tot aerumnarum finis, captivae libertas animae, periculorum evasio, depositioque oneris, debiti naturalis absolutio, finis exilii, gaudiosa repatriatio, vita immortalis? Sed et morientium quidem in morte mortis detruncatio mors est. Sane qui quo tardiore hinc morte resecantur, et plura longius gravioraque mortis opera perpetrantes acerbiore opus est morte tandem intereant, utpote durioribus excruciati suppliciis in aeternum. Hic te cupio soror meminisse jam de lauri convulsione (si somnii tamen error esse non putetur) edictum emanasse intonuisseque sententiam. Hinc eapropter conjicio ad reginam subvolatu levi mox conversa, quae deaurata vestes regis dexterae assistit varietate circumdata anachoriticam cenobitenque* atque ipsam que[17] sub mendicitatis angustiore penuria interius ita perscrutaris, ut peculiarem cuiusque austeritatem, poenitentiam perfectionemque ac varias sub uno cunctarum scopo†n† disparitates, quasi Joannis Cassiani[18] socia, non secus aperueris, ac si longevior earum in singulis domino exhibueris famulatum. Hae sunt quae ab mortis metu nos absolvunt; breviore nos calle ducunt ad patriam; gratia impinguant, augent meritis, altius promovent, redduntque de majore gloria tutissimos. Hac ego te sentio perfecta sub religionis libertate non segnius militare. Quae scrutata teipsam intimius, mensaque et corporis robur, jam mentis innixa volatibus, unde viges ipsa robustior, caelorum jam te in altissima cum hac recepisti, quae optimam quidem partem approbata est a domino delegisse. Cum deliciosi nimium exhaustique viribus, fidelis tamen hospitis tui nequeas vel fortiore satis incessu vaditare, sensisti plane quid a nobis deus maxime velit, qualesque nos gaudeat invenire. Vidisti, inquam, ubi religionis optimum delitescat, quandoquidem et quicquid ferventior extra monacus austeritatis poenitentiaeque patiatur, solius assequi ab cordis caritate meritum, ille te cordium zelator ipse docuerit. Cuius te arbitror jam amplexibus felicior infudisti. Ille igitur optimus deus, qui nemini quicquam debitor, omne liberalius bonum pro capacitatis merito singulis impartitur, quique sancto te uberius imbre compluit ex caelis gratiarum, perficiat in te quod incepit, ut in te quoque gloria illi gratiarumque actiones exolvantur a saeculis in aeternum. Vale. Pridie Id. Decembris.

Textual Notes

I.40. *citherulam*: i.e., *citharam*. | 135. *vecterinus*: i.e., *veterinus*. | 145. *denum*: i.e., *demum*. | 177. *natura*] om., Ve. | 208. *praerespuit*] *prespuit*, Vt; *perrespuit*, Ve. | 211. *extrudat*] *extendat*, Vt. | 255. *domum*] om., Vt. | 276. *actum*] *actus*, Ve. | 284. *insequitur*] *sequitur*, Ve. | 293. *syncopis*: i.e., *syncope*. | 300. *O*] *Oret*, in margin, Vt. | 301. *dicundum*: i.e., *dicendum*. | 317-18. *fratrem pullulum*] om., Vt. | 318. *abigeus*] *abigens*, Vt. | 324. *totas*] *malim totos (= se totos)*. | 329. *fortius*] *fortior*, Ve. | 337. *unda a*] *malim undam vel undas*. | 351. *impatienti*] *malim impatiens*. | 352. *quoscunque*] *quosque*, Vt. | 364. *frequentius*] om., Ve. | 383. *pertulerit*] *protulerit*, Vt. | 403. *vesper*] *malim vesperum*. | 500. *defamulatione*: i.e., *diffamulatione*. | 501. *obstringam*] *abstringam*, Vt. | 517. *inter recensendum*] *interrecendum*, Ve. | 525. *ferbesceret*: i.e., *fervesceret*. | 566. *politiei*] *malim politae*. | 566. *tenerescentiae*] *malim tenerescentis*. | 580. *epileuthicos*: i.e., *epilepticos*. | 598. *Syrtes*: i.e., *Syrtem*. | 666. *crispantium*] *crispicantium*, Vt.

II.10. *proferantur*] *proferatur*, Vt.
IV.6. *sine*] *sive*, Vt. | 17. *viscarium*] *malim viscum* (lime) *vel viscatorium* (snare).

V.1. *Catholica ecclesiae Romanae respublica*] Zanelli's text reads: *Catholica ecclesia Romana, republica*; both Vt and Ve read as above. | 9. *suscipiunt*] *suspiciunt*, Ve. | 15. *impii*] *imperii*, Vt. | 33. *sacretioribus*: i.e., *sacratioribus*. | 36. *omnipotens*] *omniparens*, Ve. | 50. *Nullus*: i.e., *Nullas*. | 52. *atque regressus*] om., Vt. | 54. *obsito*] om., Ve. | 57. *furatrinus*] *furatrivus*, Vt; also in margin, Vt.

VI.8. *videtur*] *malim videris*. | 10. *Scutrii*: i.e., *Scutari*.

VII.6. *scilice*: i.e., *silice vel scilicet*. | 7. *postero*] *malim posterius*. | 8-9. *degeneras. . .rigidior*: cf. IX. 60. | 18-20. *Ab illo. .refugis*: cf. IX. 60-62. | 22. *adjurata*: i.e., *abjurata*, Ve.

IX.9. *scalenonicam*: i.e., *scalenam*. | 15. *tripyrami*] *malim trianguli*. | 19. *orbatum*] *malim orbatus*. | 32. *sentiamur*: i.e., *sen tiamus.* | 45. *attencendarum*] *malim attentatarum.* | 48. *quas*] *malim eas.* | 65. *muneris*] *malim munere.* | 132. *qua: i.e., quae.* | 141. *aticulum*] *malim articulo.* | 143. *philomenae*: i.e., *philomelae.* | 178. *opta*: i.e., *optata.*

x.3. *obaudum] malim obaudiens vel obaudienda.* | 13. *tua*: i.e., *tua epistola.* | 33. *agnula*: i.e., a diminutive of *agnus.* | 42. *puella*: i.e., puellae. | 73. *Humilitade dico io*: Italian: "Do I say humility?" | 94. *calibea*: i.e., *caelebs.* | 94. *nexea*: i.e., *nexuosa.* | 96. *letiocula*] *malim letiofera.*

xi.1. *Escandescentia*: i.e., *Excandescentia.* | 1., 6. *nostras*: adjective, nom. sing., "native." | 23. *rinoceronthe*: i.e., *rhinocerote.* | 79. *fuerant*: i.e., *fuerint.* | 105. *frappae*: Italian, "fringe." | 117. *gracitat*] *malim gracillat.* | 147. *causare*: i.e., *causari.* | 159. *omnimode*: i.e., *omnimodo.* | 204. *bravio*: i.e., *brabeo vel brabio.* | 218. *focat*: i.e., *fucat vel focillat.* | 226. *minera*] *malim minister.* | 275. *Scaccho mato di pedone nel mezo tavolerio*: Italian: "checkmate by pawn on a chessboard." | 282. *tantin*: i.e., *tantine.* | 297. *faenera*: i.e., *faenora.*

xii.4. *gaudii*: i.e., *gaudio.* | 5. *synthomatico*: i.e., *symptomatico*, medieval Latin. | 6. *profocavit*: i.e., *provocavit.* | 9. *mitantius*: i.e., *micantius.* | 36. *anima*] MS abbreviation not clear. *Ante* fits the context. | 49. *apicula*: i.e., *apex.* | 55. *eblesulum*: i.e., *blesum.* | 59. *rhetoricen*: i.e., *rhetorices.* | 62. *pueritium*: i.e., *pueritia.* | 115. *saciasti*: i.e., *sacrasti.* | 200. *anachoriticam cenobitenque*: i.e., *anachoriticarum cenobitarumque.*

Notes to Part Three

1. A Dialogue Oration in Honor of an Ass

1. See above, Part Two, introduction to 1.

2. *Pythagoras Porphyriusque*: On Pythagoras and the idea of reincarnation see G. S. Kirk and J. E. Raven, eds., *The Presocratic Philosophers* (Cambridge University Press, 1960), fragments 268–72. Porphyry may well have been known to Cereta through Augustine, *City of God*, 10.29 or 22.12. On Porphyry see Andrew Smith, *Porphyry's Place in the Neoplatonic Tradition* (The Hague: Martinus Nijhoff, 1974), especially Chap. 4, "The Fate of the Soul after Death," pp. 56–68.

3. *adaurescat:* meaning obscure.

4. *Theocritus et Stoici atque Peripatetici*: Theocritus was a Greek bucolic poet (ca. 310–250B.C.), a number of whose poems survive. I am unaware of any attitude he expressed on the subject of the immortality of the soul, but as a pastoral poet he makes a good authority to quote as a joke on the souls of animals. The Stoics held that the soul is composed of a material substance and so perishes with the body. The Peripatetics or Aristotelians held a variety of views. Aristotle himself rejected Plato's notion of eternal ideas, on which Plato's doctrine of the immortality of the soul rested, and held that the soul is one with the body as its "form." This being the case, it is not certain that the soul survives the body in any way (*Metaphysics* 1070a). In *On the Soul*, bk. 3, however, Aristotle speaks of the passive and active intellects and suggests that the active (though not the passive) intellect survives the death of the body. Sometimes he seems to think of the active intellect as a capacity, but sometimes he speaks of it as a substance. This passage later caused splits among Aristotelians. But most of Aristotle's commentators, beginning with Alexander of Aphrodisias, were of the opinion that he did not believe in individual immortality. During the Renaissance (but after this passage in our text) Pietro Pomponazzi rejected the notion of personal immortality as an Aristotelian doctrine.

5. *Thebas Amphyon*: Amphion was the son of Antiope and Zeus. His mother, having run away from her father, was punished by imprisonment for many years by her father's brother, Lycus. When she at length escaped, she was taken under the protection of Amphion and his brother Zethus. Amphion had been given a lyre by Hermes and was

a wonderful musician. The stones of the city followed him when he played, and thus the walls of Thebes were built, a part of the story to which this passage alludes. See Apollodorus, 3.45.

6. *Gnosum Corybantes in Creta*: Cnossos was the capital of ancient Crete. The Corybantes were the priests of the goddess Cybele. I do not know of a tradition of the founding of Cnossos by the Corybantes.

7. *redibuit*: meaning obscure.

8. *grafiunt*: meaning obscure.

9. *urnipedis*: meaning obscure.

10. *bastus*: meaning obscure.

11. *Augusto aut Julio*: The references appear to be to Augustus Caesar (63 B.C.–14 A.D.) and to Julius Caesar (102–44 B.C.).

12. *Alexander . . . Bucefalo*: Bucephalus (or Bucephalas) was the favorite horse of Alexander the Great. The horse died after the battle on the Hydaspes in 326 B.C. In its memory, Alexander founded the town of Bucephala on the site. See Julius Valerius, *Res Gestae Alexandri Macedonis* 3.11.

13. *corvo*: See Pliny, *Historia naturalis* 10.43.60, par. 121 ff.

14. *Cf.* Vergil, *Aeneid*, 4.64

15. *octinundinarum*: *Nundina* means "marketplace" which seems called for here. The form as given in the text is obscure.

16. *navesque Sabini*: The Sabines lived northeast of Rome, usually in unwalled villages on the Apennine hilltops. They were gradually assimilated with the Romans. See Pliny, *Historia naturalis* 3.12.17. The *naves* here must be interpreted as land transport vehicles.

17. *dentetentimque*: This appears to be a comic word coined on the analogy of *pedetemptim*, "by feeling carefully with my teeth."

18. *ventum*: The word is used metaphorically here to mean "spirit."

19. A reference to astrology in which Cereta herself was quite accomplished. This is discussed at some length in Part One above.

20. *scalatim*: Probably "step by step."

21. *causatius*: "More effectively," medieval Latin.

22. *varios . . . strepitus*: There is no verb to govern these two accusatives. One must add, perhaps, "he feared."

23. *innixius*: "More zealously," medieval Latin.

24. *leo Nemaeus, quis Erymanthus aper, quae tigris Hyrcana*: All refer to the exploits of Hercules. See, respectively, Vergil *Aeneid* 8.295; Ovid *Metamorphoses* 5.608; Vergil *Aeneid* 4.367.

25. *pro Milone*: An extant oration Cicero actually delivered.

26. *Porciae aut censurae Semproniae sed tribunitii*: Tribunes were officers of the common people in republican Rome. A Porcian law was a law of the people's tribune. Sempronian tribunes refer to the Gracchi who first changed the law that a tribune could not be reelected.

27. *Apuleius*: The joke here is that Apuleius did honor to Asellus by changing himself into an ass.

28. *Asina*: Lewis and Short, under "Asina" mention a Cornelius Scipio Asina, referred to in Macrobius *Saturnalia* 1.6.

29. *Mavors*: A poetical name for Mars, the god of war. Also used to mean simply "war," or "battle."

30. *Plato*: See *Laws* 10.905; *Phaedo* 108, 113.
31. *Poppaea*: Wife of the Emperor Nero.
32. *Chirogricis*: Corruption for *Chiro* (genitive form *Chironis*), one among the Centaurs, possessing a special knowledge of plants, medicine, and divination. See Ovid *Metamorphoses*, 2.630 ff.
33. *pthisicus*: "illness." *phthisis*, "illness" or "consumption" in medieval Latin.
34. *Alcmaeon*: On command of his father (Amphiaraus) he killed his mother (Eriphyle) and for this reason was pursued by the Furies. See Cicero *Tusculan Disputations* 3.5.11.
35. *Sulla*: Lucius Cornelius Sulla (138–78 B.C.), Roman dictator, 88–79, B.C. He stepped down from the dictatorship, died of a disease one year later, and was given a spectacular public funeral—hardly an appropriate illustration in this context. See Sallust *Jugurthine War* 100.2.
36. *desaevit*: Perhaps an example of the heavy-handed comic touch of this oration and to be translated "rages furiously." It is unlikely that it has the unusual meaning of "ceases raging" which is found only once, in Lucretius.
37. *te haec*: Appears to be meaningless here.
38. *Quod . . . posteritas*: This entire sentence is unclear.

II. Letter to Benedict Arsagus

1. See above, Part Two, 4.

III. Letter to Benedict Arsagus

1. On this letter, see above, Part Two, 6.
2. *Pierides sive Castalides*: Names for the Muses. See Martial 9.19 and Cicero *De Natura Deorum* 3.21.54.
3. The two languages referred to here are, of course, Greek and Latin. This is one of the few indications in Cereta's letters that she knew Greek as well as Latin. See also T 17 and 36.
4. *equo Bellorophontis*: Bellerophon fought the Chimaera, the Solymi, the Amazons, and others, triumphing with the help of the winged horse Pegasus, which Athena had helped him catch. See Cicero *Tusculan Disputations* 3.26.63.

IV. Letter to Peter Serina

1. On him, see above, Part Two, introduction to 3.
2. *Idibus Augusti*: August 13 [1485]. This letter is datable with certainty. Cereta was married for only one passing of the month of August.

V. Letter to Paul Zane, Bishop of Brescia

1. On Bishop Paul Zane, see above, Part Two introduction to 19.

2. *decreti*: "Decree" or "ordinance." Here it might also mean "doctrine." The reference of the decree is not clear, but I take it to be the Roman Catholic doctrine of the Eucharist, established at the Fourth Lateran Council in 1215 and reiterated at the Council of Ferrara-Florence, where the dogma of the seven sacraments was first proclaimed.

3. *figura Mosaici serpentis*: According to Num. 21:9, Moses made a bronze serpent which, if a person were bitten by a serpent, he could look upon and live. 2 Kings 18:4 says that King Hezekiah, when he began to reign, destroyed this bronze serpent. There appears to be here an analogy, albeit vague, between the literal purpose of the Mosaic serpent and its function of guaranteeing correct belief.

4. According to a legend found in its present form in the fourteenth century, Veronica, a woman of Jerusalem, offered her headcloth to Jesus to wipe the blood and sweat from his face when he was on his way to Calvary. He returned it with his features impressed upon it. According to one version of the legend, Jesus applied the word "veronica" to the cloth, suggesting *vera eikon* ("true image") as its etymology. A portrait professing to be the original imprint seems to have been at Rome since the eighth century. It was transferred by Pope Boniface VIII to St. Peter's in 1297 and has been a highly venerated relic, especially during the fourteenth and fifteenth centuries. See the *Oxford Dictionary of the Christian Church* (London: Oxford University Press, 1958), p. 1414, where references to the literature are cited.

5. *reliquias Danaum*: This phrase in Vergil refers to the Trojan founders of Rome. The phrase is poetic, meaning "relics [or *remnants*] of the Greeks." See Vergil *Aeneid* 1.30: *Troas, reliquias Danaum atque immitis Achili.*

6. *Vestae delubro sollicitant*: Vesta was the goddess of the hearth and domestic life. The Temple of the Vestals contained no images but a perpetual fire. See Ovid Fasti 6.295–297.

7. *Colchide*: Colchis is a country on the eastern shore of the Black Sea, celebrated on account of the Golden Fleece (as here) and Medea. See Pliny *Historia naturalis* 2.103.106, par. 226.

8. *Atlantidas*: *Atlantides* would mean "the daughters of Atlas, " i.e., "the Pleiades." Perhaps, then, *apud Atlantidas* means something like "among [or *in the house of*] the daughters of Atlas."

9. Emperor Alexander Severus (222–35) is the Alexander referred to here. For this story see *Scriptores historiae Augustae*, chap. 31.

10. *Gades*: Cadiz, Spain.

11. Christian relics are likened here to the Lares, Roman household gods. The point is that if even godless pagans guard their relics, all the more should pious Christian do so. The use of *irrita figmenta* ("useless figments") suggests a certain irony in the use of *lararium*: in the shrine

of *our* household gods, we preserve relics, not of mere men, but of Christ himself.

12. *furatrinus*: patron of thieves. See Fulgentius *Mythology* 1.18.

13. The argument here, which is in part also a question, seems to be that since (through transubstantiation) the corporeal body and blood of Christ are present in the Eucharist, the possibility arises that Christ can be abused by those who unworthily steal his body and blood (for the host is left unguarded in the shrine and can be stolen). Moreover, his physical presence can be used by magicians and soothsayers for superstitious purposes (the altar can be violated at night).

14. *Pontificum decreta sanxerunt*: See above, this letter, n. 2.

15. *Undecimo Chal. Octobres.*: September 22 [1485]. Zanelli, in his article accompanying the publication of this letter (see above, reference in n. 1), believes that the letter was written under the influence of the preaching of Bernardino da Feltre and belongs to the second half of 1494. I have determined, however, that all of Cereta's letters were written by March, 1488, when she wrote her prologue dedicating this volume of her letters to Cardinal Maria Ascanio Sforza. It is placed near the beginning of the corpus in the extant sources and makes no references to the events that troubled Cereta a short time later.

VI. Letter to Helena Caesarea

1. On the correspondent and the letter, see above, Part Two, introduction to 27.

2. Cereta writes as if she were contemporary with the events she is describing here. But the incursion of which she speaks took place on the eastern coast of Italy in 1480, some years before she actually composed this letter.

3. *Constantinopolitanae cladis*: Constantinople fell to the Turks in 1453.

4. *Chalcidiique*: Chalcis, the chief city in Negroponte (Euboea), fell to the Turks in their war with Venice in 1470.

5. *Scutarii*: Scutari was twice besieged by the Turks in their war with Venice in 1477–1478. The Turks returned the city to Venice in the treaty signed between the two powers in 1479.

6. *Thrax leo*: "Thracian lion," i.e., a ferocious gladiator, but here it means "a Turkish warrior."

7. *Ninivitae*: See Jon. 3 especially 3:8.

8. *Pharaonis*: See Exod. 14:21–29.

9. *Abnegemus saeculi pompas*: Cereta wrote another letter entirely on eschewing the pomp of the world (*saeculi pompas*). See T 31: *Contra muliebrem cultum imprecatio*.

VII. Letter to Felix Tadinus

1. On this correspondent, see above, Part Two, introduction to 28.

2. *chiromantice*: A medieval Latin word which means divination by palm reading.

3. Silvester is Cereta's father and her principal teacher. The sentence may mean that he was also the teacher of Felix's son and that they have now become estranged through the actions (or perhaps the indifference) of Felix.

4. *Clarensium*: Santa Chiara was a monastery near Brescia where Cereta went regularly, perhaps for intellectual discussions. In her only extant letter to her father, T 18, she pleads with him to mediate the dispute that arose at Santa Chiara (see above, Part Two, 30). The dispute had to do with the extent of Cereta's learning, generated by jealousy of some of her contemporaries. This letter presupposes the same general situation described in the earlier one.

5. *Scythis*: The Scythians were a nomadic people who fought from horses with bows and arrows and were well versed in elusive desert tactics. In the black-earth part of Scythia, a natural wheat growing area, they exploited the labor of the previous inhabitants and sold wheat to the Greeks for Greek pottery and metalwork with which the tombs of Scythian chiefs are ornamented. The reference here may be to their general ruthlessness in battle and the fact that they made their conquered peoples work for them. See Herodotus 4.1–144.

VIII. LETTER TO MICHAEL BAETUS

1. On him, see above, Part Two, introduction to 26.

2. On her interest in astrology, see above, Part One.

3. *ac inter canes Alexandri lepuscula*: "a little rabbit among the hounds of Alexander." Perhaps a proverb.

4. *Phoebi atque Daphnes*: Daphne was changed into a laurel by the god Peneus, her father, in order to save her from the unwanted embraces of Apollo. See Ovid *Metamorphoses* I.450–590.

5. When Apollo saw that Daphne was being turned into a laurel, he lamented his lost love but declared that she would serve as his tree and that rewards for victories would come from her branches (see reference in n. 4, above). Cereta here likens herself to Daphne who preferred her freedom (Cereta her virtue) to the god Apollo, and then represents her highest happiness as that of being a maidservant (like the laurel).

6. Here Cereta begins a description of the heavens on the first four days of July, i.e., the days immediately preceding the composition of this letter, in order to prove to her correspondent that she did not get her knowledge from some book but knows how to read the zodiac herself.

IX. LETTER FROM BROTHER THOMAS OF MILAN TO SILVESTER CERETA, POEM APPENDED

1. On Brother Thomas, see above, Part Two, introduction to 49. On this letter, see above, Part Two, introduction to 68. Since the four letters written by Brother Thomas are contained only in Vt, the Vatican manuscript originally may have been that of Brother Thomas himself.

2. *attentarum infrugi rerum*: "things attempted without result."

3. In lines 66–68, Brother Thomas is literally copying from Cereta's letter to Felix Tadinus, above VII:19–20.

4. See above, Part Two, 57.

5. See above, Part Two, 29.

6. *Lucretiae . . . placavere*: "The Babylonian Lucretia," "Emilia the Amazon," and "Frederick Augustus" may be playful names for acquaintances of Cereta; she herself is called "the new Penelope" in this same sentence. The reference to the Amazon pleasing Theseus is no doubt a reference to Theseus's courtship of the Amazon Hippolyta (Antiope). See Plutarch *Theseus*, 26 ff.

7. See above, Part Two, 35, 65.

8. *Athesim*: The Adige River, near Brescia.

9. The reference is to her dialogue oration in honor of an ass. See above, Part Two, 1 and Part Three, 1.

10. See above, Part Two, 54.

11. See above, Part Two, 24,36 and 37.

12. See above, Part Two, 21.

13. See above, Part Two, 55.

14. This appears indication enough that Brother Thomas was not Cereta's teacher. He seems here to have become acquainted with her work for the first time.

15. Could it be that Vt, to which he added these letters (59, 61, 63, 65) is the copy of Cereta's letters which he looks forward to receiving?

16. Again, indication enough that Brother Thomas was never Cereta's teacher.

17. *Petrarcha*: Petrarch often contrasted the inner and outer man, e.g., in his *Ascent of Mont Ventoux*, *Secret*, and *On the Repose of the Religious*.

18. *Lynceus*: One of the argonauts, famed for his sharpness of vision. See Pindar *Nemean* 10.60.

19. *Magdalena Christo*: See Luke 8:2; Mark 15:40; 16:1 ff.; Matt. 28:9; John 20:11 ff.

20. *Petro Dorcas*: Peter raised Dorcas from the dead. See Acts 9:36–43.

21. *Drusiana Joanni*: I can find no reference to a Drusiana in biblical or patristic Christian literature.

22. *Hieronymo Paule foret aut Eustochium*: Eustochium (370–419) was a Roman virgin of noble descent. With her mother, Paula, she came under the influence of Jerome. A letter from Jerome (Ep. 22) addressed to her on the subject of virginity made it necessary for the two women to leave Rome (385). They went to Bethlehem where they built four monasteries. Paula, and after her death (404) Eustochium, governed these. See the *Oxford Dictionary of the Christian Church*, p. 476, where the literature is also cited.

23. *Scolastica fieret Benedicto*: Scholastica (480–543) was the sister of Benedict of Nursia. She is mentioned in the *Dialogues* (II.33 ff.) of Gregory the Great, the only source of our knowledge of her. She

established a convent at Plombariola, a few miles from Monte Cassino. She met with her brother annually to discuss spiritual matters.

24. *Macharii*: Macarius was a Christian apologist (fourth-fifth centuries), Bishop of Magnesia, author of an apology in five books, *Apocriticus*, attacking a Neoplatonist critic of Christianity (perhaps Porphyry). Only parts of the work survive.

25. *Antonius*: St. Antony of Egypt (251?-356), a hermit who gave away his possessions in 269 and devoted himself to a life of asceticism. In 285 he retired completely into the desert. He attracted a number of disciples and in 305 came out of his solitude to organize a community of hermits. He sided with the Athanasian party at Nicea, and Athanasius wrote his life. After the Church became the official religion of the Roman Empire, Antony's authority increased among those who resisted the secularization of the church. See *Oxford Dictionary of the Christian Church*, p. 65, where the literature is also cited.

26. I.e., Christ's ascent into heaven and His second coming.

27. *vii Idus Octobris, 1487*: October 9, 1487. This is one of only two letters in the entire Cereta corpus of 82 letters that contains a year date. The other is T 12.

28. *Taurus*: The constellation.

29. *Libra*: The constellation.

30. *Sternileum*: meaning obscure, perhaps here "sneezy."

31. *Cf.* Vergil *Aeneid*, I.123.

32. *mastrincula quercus*: "the smaller mast was of oak."

x. Letter from Brother Thomas of Milan to Laura

1. On the importance of these last three letters in interpreting Cereta's life, see Part One. On this letter, see Part Two, 72.

2. *urentius*: "more heatedly."

3. *pontica*: from the Black Sea, thus, savage and cruel, like Medea.

4. *ligustra*: meaning obscure, perhaps "plants."

5. *Paralogus*: "unexpected" or "a miscalculation."

6. *praelitura*: meaning obscure.

7. *elementatim*: "detail by detail."

8. *capinosos*: meaning obscure.

9. *Medeae*: The reference is to the fiery robe of Medea with which she poisoned the woman for whom her husband Jason left her. See Ovid *Metamorphoses* 7.396–400.

xi. Letter from Brother Thomas of Milan to Laura

1. On this letter, see above, Part Two, 74.

2. *chystifellis*: A medical term, probably from *chysto*, "red," and *fel*, "gall."

3. This is a reference to Brother Thomas's letter to Silvester. See above, ix: 137–39.

4. Cereta wrote a number of letters answering critics who contended that her father had written her letters and that a woman could not be learned. See above, Part One.

5. *Phoenice*: I.e., Phronicus, against whom Cereta wrote an invective (T 61) dated July 1 [1487].

6. There is no letter extant in which Cereta accuses Brother Thomas of having denounced her to Eusebius or Cassandra. She does accuse Boniface Bembo of doing so. See the discussion of this above, Part Two, introduction to 63.

7. She was in fact well known in Brescia. But there is no mention of her in sources from other cities (e.g., Venice) during her lifetime or shortly after her death.

8. *adolescentula*: An acknowledgement that she was still young when she wrote her letters.

9. This may be a reference to the death of her husband only eighteen months after their marriage.

10. *carmagnoleo*: meaning obscure.

11. *dissarcita*: cf. *sarcio*, "patch."

12. *stapedile*: meaning obscure.

13. *stumbulo*: meaning obscure.

14. *stupebundam*: "full of amazement."

15. *tibiones*: Perhaps "legs" or "large legs."

16. *Sfortiadas*: meaning obscure.

17. *subimo*: Perhaps "beneath."

18. *supplexa*: "well-broken horse."

19. This appears to be a dig at Cereta's astrological interests.

20. Another dig, this time at Cereta's oration in honor of an ass. Here and above (n. 19) she is being equated with pompous rhetoricians.

21. *decaputiatus*: "bareheaded."

22. Aristotle *Posterior Analytics* I.6.74b; I.33.88b; *passim*.

23. In a letter published in Tomasini from Cereta to Brother Thomas, she protests that she is not concerned with deducing abstract truths of the nature described here, implying that she felt herself implicated by this charge. See T 52, pp. 114–15.

24. *vaditare*: frequentative of *vadare*, "to wade through."

25. *napellorum*: "monkshood," a botanical term (medieval).

26. *Herostrato*: The Ephesian who set fire to the Temple of Diana in Ephesus in order to become famous. See Solinus 40.3.

27. At the beginning of his life of Alexander, Plutarch says that the Temple of Diana of Ephesus was burned on the night Alexander was born but that the goddess was not there because she was assisting in the birth of Alexander. Diana is called Lucina in her capacity as helper at childbirth.

28. *obnubilatione*: post-classical, "darkening," "clouding." See Augustine, *Miscellanea Agostiniana* (Rome, 1930), p. 336.15.

29. Cereta asked this in T 56, p. 130.

30. This, I think, is clear evidence that Brother Thomas was not Cereta's teacher. No teacher would have said this, especially to a young girl.

31. *scachorum*: Medieval Latin, from *scacci*, "chessmen."
32. *gogulus*: meaning obscure, perhaps *gloriosus* is intended.
33. *Phocion*: An Athenian general and statesman of the fourth century B.C. He advocated preserving peace with Philip of Macedon and was befriended by him and later by Philip's son Alexander. When democracy was restored Phocion was put to death by the Athenians (318). The story referred to by Brother Thomas is told in Plutarch's *Life of Phocion* 21.

XII. Letter from Brother Thomas of Milan to Laura

1. On this letter, see above, Part Two, 75.
2. *Digitari*: Medieval Latin, "to point out."
3. *pavidule*: Medieval Latin, "fearfully."
4. *cranevacuum*: "empty head."
5. *palpulam*: a female flatterer, a "soft-touch."
6. *enuntiaria*: Apparently an adjective coined from the verb *enuntio*.
7. Iphigenia restored Cimon, a Florentine, to sanity, and made him famous. Brother Thomas may be using mythological names in code to refer to contemporary citizens.
8. *postergantem*: "putting in its wake."
9. *remigulus*: "an oarsman."
10. *cymba*: "a skiff."
11. *Deodati*: Perhaps a reference to Augustine's son Adeodatus. See Augustine *Confessions* 9.6.14.
12. *magnipensio*: Medieval Latin, "high esteem."
13. One year before this letter was written (1486), Giovanni Pico della Mirandola had published his 900 theses preceded by his *Oration on the Dignity of Man*, widely circulated at the time. This is doubtless a reference to Pico's treatise which was only the latest and strongest expression of a theme that can be found in a number of Quattrocento humanists. See on this, Charles Trinkaus, *In our Image and Likeness*, 2 vols. (Chicago: University of Chicago Press, 1970).
14. *stomachosa*: Medieval, not the classical, form: "stomach."
15. *Sed hospite destituatur*: "But it [the body] may be deprived of its host," i.e., one may die.
16. *Noctem . . . auroram*: Sense of this in relation to the preceding sentence requires the order *auroram . . . noctem*.
17. *que*: obscure.
18. *Joannis Cassiani*: John Cassian (360–435) participated in the monastic movement in both the East and the West. He settled in the West around 400 and subsequently wrote two books for which he is best known: *Institutes*, which sets out rules for monastic life and discusses the eight hindrances to a monk's perfection, and was taken as the basis for a number of western rules, including that of Benedict; and his *Conferences*, which recount his conversations with the great leaders of eastern monasticism. See the *Oxford Dictionary of the Christian Church*, p. 243, where the literature is cited.

Index of Names

Laura Cereta of Brescia, one of the few women of letters in the fifteenth century, was an enthusiastic Humanist, thoroughly educated in Latin and Greek, a woman of wit and perception, and a sharp critic of the antifeminism so prevalent in her society. Professor Rabil's book consists of three parts: (i) an analysis of her life and thought, based on all the extant sources; (ii) a study of the sources, a dating of the letters, and a table showing the relationship between Tomasini's 1640 edition and the manuscripts, and (iii) a critical edition of the eleven unpublished letters and one mock funeral oration in honor of an ass. The four letters to her from her spiritual counselor (here published for the first time) are indispensable for interpreting the later years of her life.

Albert Rabil, Jr., is Distinguished Teaching Professor of Humanities at the State University of New York, Old Westbury. Among his awards are a Union Seminary Traveling Fellowship, a Kent Fellowship, a Fulbright Grant, and the Columbia University Ansley Award. His major works include *Erasmus' Paraphases of Romans and Galations* (forthcoming, Univ. of Toronto Press, 1981?), *Erasumus and the New Testament: The Mind of a Christian Humanist* (Trinity Univ. Press: San Antonio, 1972), and *Merleau-Ponty: Existentialist of the Social World* (Columbia Univ. Press, 1967). He has published a number of articles as well.

mrts

medieval & renaissance texts & studies *is a research program and publication program of CEMERS, the Center for Medieval and Early Renaissance Studies at the State University of New York at Binghamton. The main* **mrts** *series emphasizes texts, translations, and major research tools. From time to time distinguished monographs and reprints will also be published.* **mrts** *is also engaged in the adaptation of modern technology for scholarly purposes and in fostering new approaches to scholarly publication.*